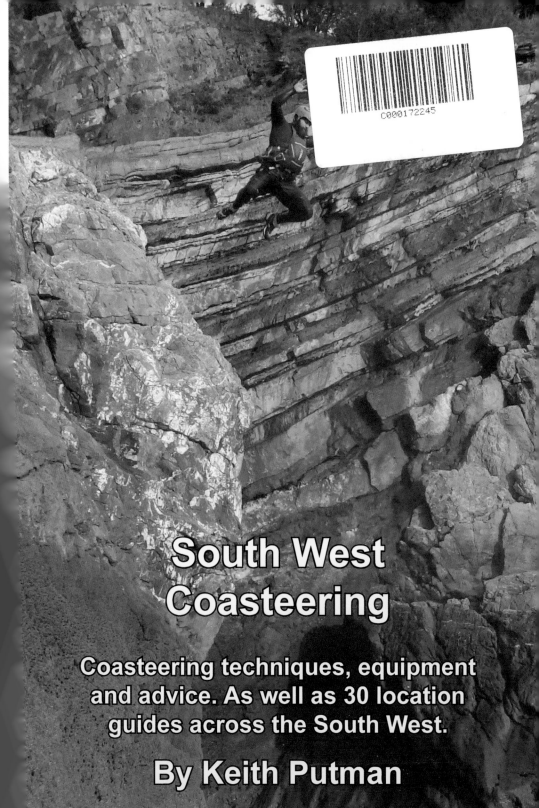

South West Coasteering

Coasteering techniques, equipment and advice. As well as 30 location guides across the South West.

By Keith Putman

Copyright © Keith Putman 2016
First edition 2016
Published by: Keith Putman
Photography by Keith Putman or Go Coasteering unless stated
For More info visit www.gocoasteering.com

ISBN 978-0-9954908-0-2

Acknowledgements
Coasteering is not a solo activity and the following people have got tired, cold and sea worn with me. Special thanks to my understanding and patient family - Katy, Lily and Evie. A big thanks to Mick Burke at Soggy Lemming for his support and excellent photography.

Mick Burke, Ian Stocker, Andrew Brierley, Paul Madeley, Maddy Williams, James Andrews, Dave Edmonds, Jon Gunn, Ben Bird, Adam Kendrick, Aaron Daeche, Matt Thomas, Phil Sage, Simon Dolphin, Nicky Selby, Caroline Stocker and anyone else that came along on one of the many trips.

Contents

The Guides

Introduction

Coasteering has grown immensely in the last 5 years. More and more people are using coasteering for stag and hen parties, birthdays, corporate team building and keeping fit. It is also growing popular with enthusiasts from other adventure sports like kayaking and climbing. I set out to write this book to provide people with the basic knowledge and skills to enjoy the sport safely and also to save them hours of time trying to find somewhere to go. The book is a selection of the best venues in the Southwest. There are plenty of other spots to find and explore. Although a book can never replace time in the water with a trained guide, it will hopefully introduce more people to the sport in a safe way.

What is Coasteering?

Coasteering opened up a whole world of new adventures for me. The coastline feels like unexplored territory even though every inch of it has been seen by boat or kayak. It gives you an extreme close up of some outstanding locations that are rarely visited. Even if the beach is mobbed by tourists a short scramble, swim and jump will take you somewhere completely deserted. Sea caves, rock arches and sea creatures are only the beginning. The sea brings its own challenges and dangers. Coasteering is as much about negotiating these as about jumping from height. Coasteering can be done by anyone and this freedom is what is attracting so many to the sport. The equipment is simple and relatively cheap and previously visited venues can hold new challenges in different conditions.

How To Use This Book

The first part of this book is full of advice and techniques to help you get into coasteering. The aim is to give you an introduction to the essential skills and equipment you will need to have a safe sea adventure. The skills and techniques described take practise and understanding. We recommend you contact a coasteering provider to seek further advice and training to enable you to really enjoy coasteering safely.

The Guides

The second part of this book is a guide to 30 locations across Devon ,Cornwall and Dorset. This is the tip of the iceberg; the South West has hundreds of amazing places to explore through coasteering but I hope this gives you somewhere to begin. Each guide has grid references for parking, starting and finishing points and each map is designed to be used alongside a 1:25000 ordinance survey map. Each guide also has a quick reference section to give you a feel for the location.

Difficulty

The guides are split into 3 difficulty categories:

Beginner - These trips are great for people new to coasteering. Usually sheltered with easy entry and exit points.

Intermediate - Expect less sheltered water, harder climbs, longer swims, potentially risky currents and rips. Knowledge of sea conditions and features are required.

Expert - These trips usually have very few entry and exit points, they are exposed and dangerous areas to be in. A good knowledge of all aspects of the sport and plenty of experience will make these trips fun, safe and exciting.

Other Symbols

 Tide Time - The number of hours before high water when the route is best. Keep in mind that this is a guide and that the height of any tide will depend on spring and neap tides as well as weather conditions.

 Swell Height - This is a rough maximum swell height for the route.

 Adverse Wind or Swell Direction - Wind or swell coming from the direction indicated could cause rough conditions even in sheltered locations.

 Jump Height- The biggest jump heights on the route. Jump heights will depend on tide and whether you are telling stories in the pub.

 Route Length - The length of the coasteering route. This does not include the walk in or out.

  Walking Distance - The Distance to and from the car park to the entry and exit points

  Grid Reference - Grid references for the entry and exit points.

Useful Terminology

Zawn - A deep and narrow sea inlet, especially Cornwall and the South West, cut by erosion into sea cliffs and with steep or vertical side walls.

Sump - An underwater swim through a cave or under a boulder.

Map Guide

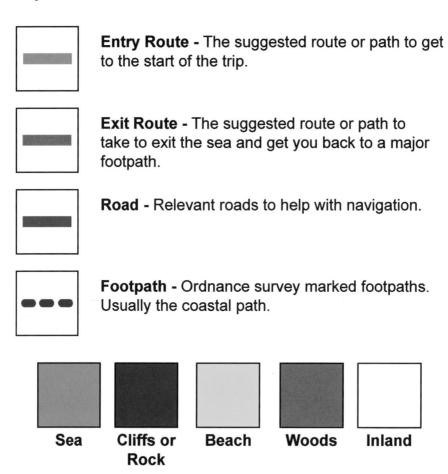

Entry Route - The suggested route or path to get to the start of the trip.

Exit Route - The suggested route or path to take to exit the sea and get you back to a major footpath.

Road - Relevant roads to help with navigation.

Footpath - Ordnance survey marked footpaths. Usually the coastal path.

Sea   **Cliffs or Rock**   **Beach**   **Woods**   **Inland**

®SoggyLemming

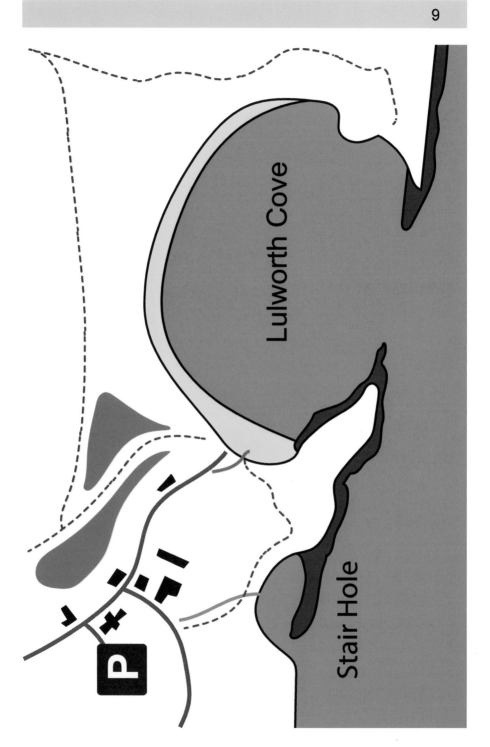

Lulworth Cove

Stair Hole

Wetsuit - Protects you from the cold and abrasions

Helmet - Full cut with ear protection

Buoyancy Aid - Vest style with attached knife and whistle

Gloves - Neoprene or mountain bike style gloves

Rescue Belt - Releasable throw line and tow line

Shorts - Protect your suit and make you look cool

Footwear - Study trainers with wetsuit socks

Clothing and Equipment

The equipment you need to coasteer safely and comfortably is relatively cheap compared to other adventure sports. There are many alternatives and personal preference plays a big part.

Wetsuits

Wetsuits work by insulating your body from the cold water on the outside of the suit. Nitrogen bubbles in the material do most of this insulation, the thin layer of water between you and the suit only provides small amounts of insulation. Wetsuits are essential for coasteering even in the warmer summer months. Apart from warmth, they also provide protection from barnacles and they will provide some buoyancy.

Fitting

A tight fitting wetsuit will trap a small amount of cold water which is slightly heated by your body heat. A baggy wetsuit will allow cold water to keep filling your suit robbing you of precious body heat - this is known as flushing. The seal around your neck, ankles and wrists should also be tight to prevent this.

Thickness

All wetsuits leak heat, the amount of heat will depend on the thickness. A 3mm wetsuit is stretchy and light which makes swimming and climbing easier. A 5mm suit will restrict you but you lose a lot less body heat. It's a personal choice but most people have 2 suits, one for summer and one for winter.

Buoyancy Aids

Buoyancy aids are personal floatation devices used in many water sports. The amount of buoyancy they add will depend on the size and type but most manufactures will have a guide to help you choose the right size and fit. Although they can be restrictive, they give us many advantages while coasteering:

- In big swell it will keep your head out of the water and stop you dunking
- They add further insulation keeping you warmer
- They can act like a harness while towing or lifting casualties
- You can jump into shallower water
- They protect you from impact and abrasion
- You can be lazy and float around while taking pictures

What Type?

There is a vast choice of manufacturer and type. As long as it fits properly, is in good condition and has the right amount of buoyancy for your size and weight then the choice is yours.

Impact Vest	**Centre BA**	**White Water BA**
Designed for sailing, these vests are warm, light and non restrictive but have limited flotation.	Designed for all sorts of canoeing and water sports activities. The buoyancy aid vest is non restrictive and tight fitting.	Designed for white water. They can be bulky but you get extra buoyancy and a handy pocket.

Helmets

Helmets will protect you from rock fall and impact when the swell is hammering you. Choose a water sports helmet that is light, comfortable and fits. You do not want your helmet slipping forwards or backwards, exposing your head to danger.

Full Cut Helmet
The full cut will also protect the back of your head and ears.

Half Cut Helmet
The half cut gives you adequate protection from above and to your forehead.

Peaked
Avoid peaked helmets. When you hit the water the peak catches and can you give you whiplash.

Footwear

Your choice of footwear is very important. You need something to climb in, swim in, walk in and keep you warm. Here are some popular options:

- **Wetsuit boots** - They keep you warm and have a sticky sole but they are flimsy and do not offer much protection
- **Trainers** - Fell running shoes are good as they drain fast and offer you protection. Wear a neoprene sock to keep your feet warm
- **Canyon or River Boot** - There are boots available that are designed for kayaking and canyoning that suit coasteering too. They are warm and offer protection as well as having great soles. They can be expensive though

Gloves

Gloves can be worn to keep you warm and protected. Some people find them too restrictive when climbing but barnacles are sharp. Neoprene gloves will keep you warm but they wear out quickly. Some providers offer gloves designed for handling glass which offer protection from barnacles. Mountain bike style gloves also work well. If you regularly go coasteering your hands do get used to the abuse and as your technique gets better, you get less damage to your hands.

Safety Equipment

Like any adventure sport carrying a small amount of safety equipment and learning how to use it can save lives. There are numerous ways to carry this equipment, in buoyancy aid pockets, dry bags or using releasable belts. It comes down to personal preference and your experiences of using the equipment.

Rescue Belt

A rescue belt is one way to carry your throw line and tow line. There are other methods but keeping them on a releasable belt grants you quick access and does not interfere with swimming, jumping or climbing.

Throw Line

A throw line is a bag filled with a length of floating rope. You can buy these in any good kayak shop. The length of your line will depend on preference but a 15m line should be sufficient. A knife should always be at hand when using ropes.

Tow Line

Having something to tow a tired or impaired swimmer is very useful. There are many options to choose from:

- **A rescue belt with built in tow line** - Easy access and non restrictive
- **A 5m sling and karabiner carried in a buoyancy aid pocket** - Can make your buoyancy aid bulky when climbing and swimming but is very versatile
- **A rescue tube** - Often carried by beach lifeguards. A great visual aid and easy to tow with but restrictive and bulky

Mobile Phone

A mobile phone is a very useful tool. You can contact emergency services who can then track you via the phone and you can use the GPS features to track your position and record your route. I buy a cheap but sturdy pay as you go phone and keep it in a waterproof case. There are a variety of cases on the market but I recommend a solid camera style case.

Knife and Whistle

The sea is loud and whistles are another way to communicate with group members or rescue services. An easily accessible knife is a must when carrying throw lines and tow lines, it is also handy for making your sandwiches.

First Aid Kit

A small simple first aid kit carried in the group is enough to deal with a large portion of coasteering injuries. Attending a first aid course will give you the skills and knowledge to decide what to carry and how to use it.

Planning Your Trip

Just like any other adventure sport, coasteering requires some planning and preparation to keep you safe and to make the most out of your trips. The sea is a constantly changing environment and a good understanding of some basic concepts will help greatly with venue and route choice.

Tides

When we are planning our trip, the tides will dictate where we go and at what time we get there. Getting this right is important so we can have fun, safe trips. This section explains the basics of tides and tidal planning. This is not a comprehensive guide to tides but it covers the basic information you need to start planning trips. Tides are caused by the gravitational force between the earth, sun and moon. The relative positions of the of earth, sun and moon also create Spring and Neap tides. The moon, being closer to the earth has the most effect, but the position of the sun will increase or decrease this.

Spring Tides

When the sun, moon and earth are aligned we have a strong combined force creating large tides.
Spring tides occur twice a month, on a new moon and a full moon. With springs we get a big tidal range. High water (HW) is higher and low water (LW) is lower. This means our landings could be shallower or the jump could not exist at all. There are also larger amounts of water moving around which can cause rips and strong currents.

New Moon

Full Moon

Neap Tides

When the moon is at right angles to the earth, the gravitational pull of the moon still creates a high water but the suns pull cancels some of it out, giving us small tides.

Neap tides also occur twice a month, on the 1st and 3rd quarter of the moon. A neap tide means low high water and high low water. The range is smaller, therefore we have more flexibility when choosing where to go and there is less water moving around.

 First Quarter

 Third Quarter

Moon Phases

Tide Timetables

Tide timetables contain most of the information we need to plan our trip. You can get this information from local surf/fishing shops in little books, the internet (www.easytide.co.uk), nautical almanacs and various mobile phone apps (boatie, world tides). Remember that most timetables in the UK are based on GMT or UTC time zones. Between March 30th and October 26th (British Summer Time) you will need to add an hour.

Tidal Range

Neaps and Springs can have a huge effect on the height of jumps and depth of landings. The height difference between low and high water gives us our tidal range.

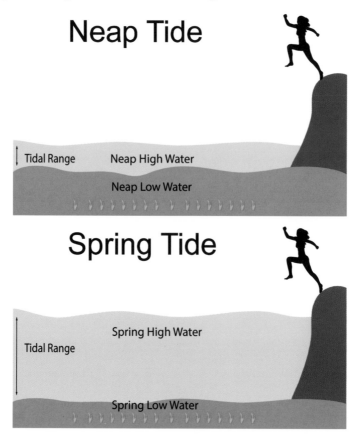

Neap Tide

Tidal Range   Neap High Water

Neap Low Water

Spring Tide

Tidal Range

Spring High Water

Spring Low Water

Rule of Twelfths

The rule of twelfths is a way to predict the height of the tide at any hour. Some venues will only work at certain tide heights so this is a useful tool.

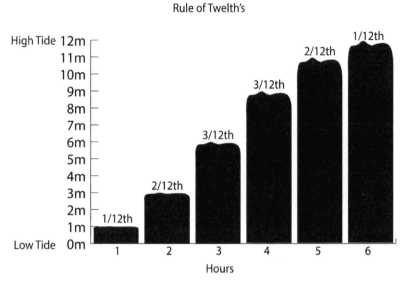

Rule of Twelth's

The range of this tide is 12m. In the 3rd and 4th hours we have half of the total amount of water moving (6 twelfths of the tidal range). This is when the tide is strongest. The tide then slows until it reaches High Water.

Wind and Swell

Before we go on any coasteering trip we need to find out what the sea conditions are and think about how they will affect our chosen venue. A big swell and breaking waves will produce a completely different trip to a calm day. Big swell will limit your entry and exit points, make it hard to swim and it can throw you around like a rag doll.

Forecasts

There are numerous ways to get accurate wind and swell forecasts for coasteering. The inshore shipping forecast from the met office and a good surfing website like **www. magicseaweed.co.uk** are the most useful. From your chosen surf report website we can get predicted swell height and direction, wind direction and speed, tide times and weather forecasts. All of this information will add to your choice of venue for the day.

Start Point to Lands End	
12:00 UTC 5th March to 12:00 UTC 6th March	
Wind	Northwesterly
Sea State	Moderate
Weather	Showers
Visibility	Good

The inshore waters forecast gives us the sea conditions from the coastline to 12 miles offshore. To read them we need to know a bit of the jargon. The wind section gives us the direction the wind is coming from and the force of it. This uses the Beaufort wind scale. The sea state section is described according to the Douglas Sea Scale.

Force	Speed in Knots	Description	Sea Description	Sea State	Coasteering
0	0	Calm	Flat like a mirror	Calm	Sea is easier to exit and features are less powerful
1	1 - 3	Light Air	Ripples, no foam	Smooth	Sea is easier to exit and features are less powerful
2	4 - 6	Light Breeze	Smooth wavelets, not breaking	Smooth	Features start to form
3	7 - 10	Gentle Breeze	Large wavelets. Crests begin to break. White horses	Slight	Swimming becomes more difficult. Jump heights vary and exiting the water is harder
4	11 - 16	Moderate Breeze	Small waves, more frequent white horses	Moderate	Swimming is difficult. Entering and exiting the water requires timing and technique
5	17 - 21	Fresh breeze	Moderate waves. Long and pronounced. Some spray	Rough	Waves crash on the cliffs. Features become powerful and coasteering is difficult and dangerous.

The Beaufort scale combined with the Douglas scale, with the final column describing how it can effect coasteering. The Beaufort scale goes up to 12 but anything above force 5 is probably too rough.

Jumping Techniques

To Jump or Not to Jump?

There are many considerations to take into account before we choose to jump off a ledge or cliff edge. Jumping from any height can have serious consequences, from a 10m jump you will be hitting the water at around 30mph. Most of the dangers involved can be avoided by making good decisions and using correct technique. This can be a complicated choice and it has many factors which affect your decision. We can make this easier by answering three questions: Can I safely get to the jump? Is the landing area safe? Is the take-off clean? The following sections will help you answer these questions.

State of Mind

Most people have a natural fear of heights. How we cope with that fear and how extreme it is will greatly effect our decision to jump. In most cases it is something that we get better at the more we are exposed to it. Other things which will affect that fear are:

- **Experience** - An experienced coasteerer will have been exposed to heights regularly and will use this to gauge if the jump is within their limits. A bad experience at height e.g. a bad landing or take off, could prevent the person from doing jumps that are within their abilities. Starting on small jumps and increasing height as confidence grows is a great way to get that good experience we all want

- **Peers** - How our peers think of us is a big factor. A negative aspect is that some people will feel they have to go off a jump just because everyone else has or they will fear the verbal abuse if they wimp out. Conversely our peers can support us positively, and our friends will know the right things to say to coach us and help control that fear

Landing Area

We need to check that our landing area is deep enough, clear of obstacles and wide enough. The height of the jump, equipment worn, your weight and how you land will all affect the depth needed for the jump. Protruding rocks and ledges are the most common obstacles, although fishing debris and litter can be an issue. Experience will help you judge the depth you will need but the following techniques can be useful too.

- In good visibility use a dive mask to see what lurks beneath.

- Dunk a friend, push them down with your feet. As a rough guide you will need 3m of depth for a 6m jump

- Scout the venue at a spring low tide to see any rocks or obstacles that may be hidden.

Take Off Area

We need to think about the size of our take-off area but more importantly we need to look at the approach to it. Pick a take-off area which is within your ability to climb up to and take into consideration the consequences of a slip or fall during your climb. If the jump height or landing is on the edge of your ability, consider how easy it would be to down climb from the take off. Loose slippery rock on take off can cause some serious jumping errors.

Some take off ledges are big enough for multiple jumpers.

How to Jump

Here are a few top tips to help you get a clean take-off and a safe pain free landing.

The Launch

Putting the right amount of energy into your jump comes with experience and is also dictated by your landing area. A good solid front leg to launch you out will give you the control and momentum you will need. Avoid a run up as this will increase your risk of slipping.

Falling

This should be the easiest bit of jumping but being unstable and out of control in the air is the cause of many painful landings. People have numerous ways of controlling themselves in the air but the key principles are momentum and stability.
Having forward momentum rather than upwards momentum whilst falling helps you maintain stability in air. Make a big star jump shape in the air, pushing your chest out. Try and keep this shape for along as possible in the air. This will stop your body rotating or leaning on the way down. A rigid body shape can cause you to lose your balance in the air which will mean a painful landing.

Landing

A good launch and a stable position in the air will take most of the challenge out of landing. Just before you hit the water close your shape bringing in your arms and legs to land two footed. Keeping your arms crossed or tight to your side will prevent any shoulder damage or your hands slapping on the water surface, ouch.

Safety and Rescue

Coasteering is an adventure activity and because of the environment we operate in we need to have the equipment and knowledge to deal with an incident. This knowledge is best gained from talking to your local coasteering provider and organising a course but here are some tips on using the equipment.

Towing Aids

Sometimes a simple tow can help massively. Tired or injured people may just need a hand into the beach or side to catch their breath before moving on. Whichever system you choose must be simple and effective.

Sling Tow -Thread your line or sling through the shoulder straps of the persons buoyancy aid and clip the karabiner to the rope. This can then attach to your throw bag belt which gives you distance from them and the ability to quick release

Arm Tow-Thread your arm through the buoyancy aid strap and tow with a side stroke. It is simple and easy to set up. You can also have a chat as you go

Throw Lines

A 15m throw line can be an extremely handy rescue aid while coasteering. A quick release belt of some kind is an ideal way of carrying it. Throw lines can be used in many situations but it takes practise and training to use efficiently and safely. Here are some tips on aiding a tired or impaired swimmer into the side or beach:

- Decide where you want them to end up. Look for easy exit points
- Look for any obstacles between you and them
- Communicate with them so they are aware of your plans
- Throw your rope with one hand while holding the end of the line with the other. There are many ways of throwing a line, training and practise is required
- Managing them on the line is difficult because they will be moving up, down, forward , backwards and sideways depending on the sea movement
- Keep an eye on any loose rope to ensure it is not getting snagged or in your way
- The person needs to stay in contact with the rope, facing the thrower so they can receive instructions and prepare to use their legs to fend off the cliff side and aid in exiting the water.
- The force on the thrower can pull them in. Sit down and get someone to support you

Dorset

The limestone and chalk cliffs of Dorset make up a large part of the Jurassic Coast, England's first natural world heritage site. The scenic rock formations and sheltered bays provide us with a few coasteering gems. Although there is not a huge selection of venues, a coasteering trip to Dorset will not disappoint.

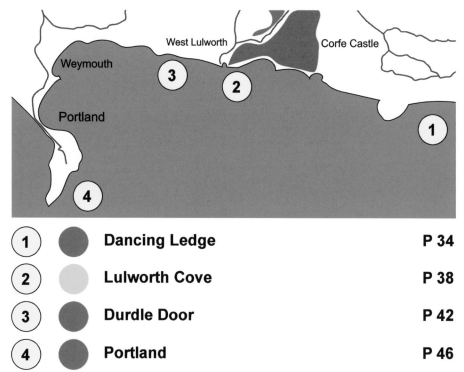

1	●	**Dancing Ledge**	**P 34**
2	○	**Lulworth Cove**	**P 38**
3	●	**Durdle Door**	**P 42**
4	●	**Portland**	**P 46**

Dancing Ledge

Dancing Ledge is one of the few points at which you can access the sea along this coastline. It is an ideal venue if you love exploring sea caves. There are numerous warning signs informing you of the dangerous rock fall in the area, these are not just for show so beware. Outside the set route are several bird ban restrictions. Please research this before heading further afield.

Approach

Follow the A351 from Wareham or Swanage then turn off on the B3069 towards Langton Matravers. In the centre of the village turn onto Dunford Drive, there are signs pointing to Langton Manor. Continue down the road past the swanky Manor and park at the end of the lane. The walk from here is well signed, just follow the big tracks. Follow the signs to Dancing Ledge all the way and a short scramble down brings you to the huge ledge.

500m   1.5km   1.5km   2   0.5m   10m

Entry / Exit
SY 997 769

Car Park
SY 997 783

Post Code
BH19 3HG

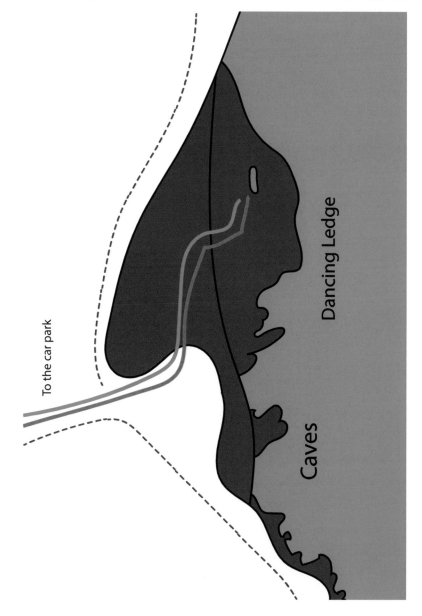

To the car park

Dancing Ledge

Caves

Description

You can reach the sea by scrambling down from the ledge in the far left corner. Here there is a large sloping slab, swell smashes onto this in rough conditions and can wash off the unwary. If you head East you will find a small cave with some worthwhile traversing but little else, most of the action is to the West. Moving along under Dancing Ledge there are plenty of smaller 2-4m jumps and gullies to warm up on. As the ledge finishes the cliffs get bigger and you will notice the bay and caves. You can jump into the bay from ledges dotted around although the landings are only deep between the boulders that linger on the seabed. A clear flat day is the best time for your first visit.

The caves are the main feature of this trip and the first set starts here. Enter through a narrow slot then swim around the back of the huge boulders and mount a narrow gap to escape out into the open. There is now a jumble of boulders which form a spit before you get to the next bay. There are a few jumps around this point but the best ones are difficult to climb onto. The next set of caves are the best. Enter to the right of a huge limestone rib which separates the cave further in. Explore the many holes, exits and entrances. At higher water you can swim under the rib and into the next cave, scary. At the exit to the caves are a few hard to reach ledges which you can jump from if you can pick out the deeper areas. After this the trip fizzles out and there are bird bans between March 1st and July 31st which could prevent any further exploration. A short swim across the bays will get you back to the start.

Lulworth Cove

Photo by SP Ingram

Lulworth Cove is a popular area with many attractions, not just the exciting coasteering. The cove can get very busy during the holidays but is well worth the visit. This trip is riddled with caves and sumps, however not all of them are friendly especially with a swell running.

Approach

Lulworth Cove is hard to miss with clear signposts from Dorchester and Poole. Follow the A352(Dorchester) or the A351(Poole) to the B3071 and follow this to Lulworth Cove. The car park is massive, so find somewhere to park and get geared up here. The start is an impressive rock feature called Stair Hole. From the car park walk towards the beach and turn right at the visitor centre, Stair Hole is 100m further on.

	700m	200m	200m			0.5m	15m
	Entry	Exit		Car Park		Post Code	
	SY 822 799	SY 824 799		SY 822 801		BH20 5RQ	

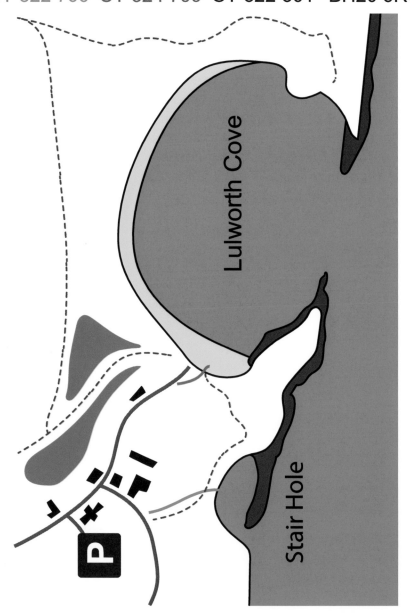

Lulworth Cove

Stair Hole

P

Description

Stair Hole has too many great jumps, climbs and caves to describe them all. The best jumps are earned by some tricky climbing. To kick start the trip climb up the face of the main cave to reach a very photogenic 5m jump over the cave mouth. Climb up over the slot to jump into the cave. The main cave contains 4-5 good jumps and lots of traversing and climbs. Explore the small holes cautiously as they go very deep and a big set can fill them with water quickly. At lower tides you can follow these caves all the way through to the opposite cave. Once you have exhausted Stair Hole start you journey east along the main cliff. The next 200m is covered in good climbing and big jumps into deep water. Harder climbing rewards you with some of the best jumps. From here the only escape routes are back the way you came or to carry on to Lulworth Cove.

If you carry on you are rewarded with the zawn crack section. This zawn contains Burke's sump and a big 10-12m jump. Burke's sump is a fantastic 3m underwater swim through the limestone hole, I recommend you have someone ready to pull you through just in case. If the sump didn't give you enough of a buzz, easily scramble up to the big overhanging jump. A mixture of traversing and swimming will bring you to the end of the high cliffs and into the protection of the cove. This last section is plagued with suck holes and caves which could be dangerous if a person was caught unaware. In flat conditions you can swim through the largest of these, amazing fun. Once in the cove walk 200m through the village back to the car park for tea and medals.

Durdle Door

Durdle Door is a huge scenic limestone arch just south of Lulworth Cove. It's an extremely popular tourist attraction with ample parking and in rough conditions Man O' War Cove can still be very sheltered so there is always something to do here. Most of the bigger jumps do require some climbing skill but do not let this put you off going to this amazing location.

Approach

From the A352 turn off at the Red Lion Hotel onto Water Lane. This is signposted Lulworth Cove. Drive for 3miles until you reach the Durdle Door Holiday Park. Drive through the park to the big public car park. Bring lots of change. The footpath down to the arch and Man o' War Cove is huge and hard to miss. Man o' War Cove is the large sandy beach to your left, I recommend starting at the end of this beach and traversing the line of rocks which protect the cove.

Entry	Exit	Car Park	Post Code
SY 809 802	SY 805 802	SY 810 805	BH20 5PU

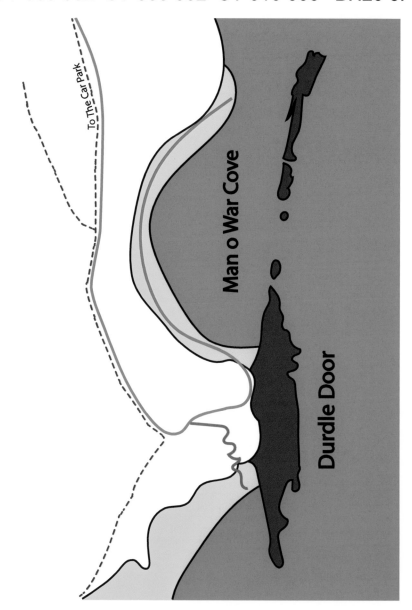

Description

Starting at the far end of Man O' War Cove, swim out into the sheltered bay onto the start of the ridge that runs all the way along the cove. Even in rough conditions this ridge line can protect the cove from the worst of it. The waves crash over it as you traverse along and the odd one will wash you off if your timing is out. In flat calm conditions this is also a great place to be and a bit of sun makes it feels like some kind of Hollywood set. There are lots of small jumps off the ridge but be aware of hidden spikes of rock. At the end of the ridge you will need to swim 20m between the isolated island of rock and the beginning of the main headland itself. In big conditions this swim can be quite an adventure.

The traverse around to the arch is 250m long and very exposed
to crashing swell. This is where the bigger jumps start . Straight
away you will find a big ledge with some 2-4m jumps which is
easy to approach. Above the next small bay is a fantastic 7-9m
jump. Climb up the slope on grippy limestone to the small take
off. Traverse around the corner and into the cave hole which
you can enter via a small jump to the left. In the hole there is
a blow hole to left which can be powerful in rough conditions.
In the back of the cave you have two testing features, the
chimney which leads to a platform above the cave or the 5m
sump which leads back the way you came (it's best to do this
in flat conditions with a mask). Once out of the hole continue
scrambling along and up to a 10m spike with a large platform.
There are plenty of take off points along here to leap from. The
next 100m are fairly uneventful until you get to the arch itself,
keep an eye out for the impressive fossils on route. As you
come round the corner onto Durdle Door itself you cannot help
but be impressed by the massive arch. The far side of the arch
has some great climbs up to exciting jumps. To finish, swim to
the beach, push through the crowds and head back to the main
path.

Portland Bill

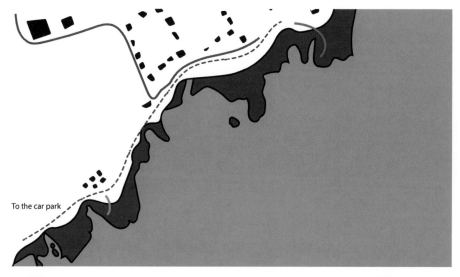

To the car park

Entry	Exit	Car Park	Post Code
SY 679 685	SY 682 687	SY 677 685	DT5 2JT

Portland Bill is the headland of the Isle of Portland, famous for its lighthouse. The area was heavily used for quarrying and a large amount of the sea bed is littered with the rock debris. The jumps are not huge and it is a short trip but the caves and scenery make up for this easily. This is a very exposed piece of coast so it's recommended that the sea is dead calm for this trip.

Approach

Drive onto the island on the A354 then follow the many signs to Portland Bill. The car park is hard to miss, you could land planes on it. From here walk 200m along the East side of the island until you reach a jumble of buildings and a boat hoist.

The starting point is one of the best jumps of the trip. It's a 6m jump into a narrow but deep zawn. It's worth scrambling back up to do it again. The traversing underneath the boat hoist is challenging but enjoyable and this leads to a large flat slab. Quickly move over the slab to get to the more interesting sections that follow. The next 100m consists of low traversing and series of connected caves which are amazing fun to crawl around in. On the next promontory of land there are small ledges to climb up to and leap off. The landings get shallow quickly around mid tide. Big caves and a warren of holes and scrambles follow until you reach another large slab. This would be a very intimidating place to be in any swell. The next 100m holds little interest until you reach the large zawn and slab which indicates the end of the trip. There are some final jumps here to exhaust yourself on before the easy scramble back to the coastal path.

South Devon is also known as the English Riviera and for good reason. Many of these venues are sheltered and are a good option when the North Coast is big. Calm seas, outstanding scenery, big rock arches, a variety of jumps and plenty of wildlife make this a fantastic area for coasteering.

South Devon

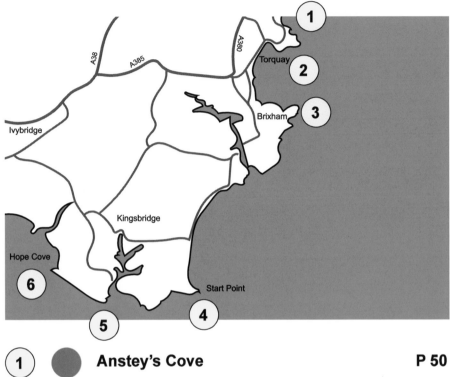

1	●	**Anstey's Cove**	**P 50**
2	○	**Daddyhole**	**P 56**
3	●	**Brixham**	**P 60**
4	○	**Start Point**	**P 64**
5	○	**Starehole Bay**	**P 68**
6	●	**Hope Cove**	**P 72**

Anstey's Cove

Anstey's Cove is a very sheltered and easily accessible venue. It has something for everybody, jumps both big and small, great sea level traversing and a licensed café for afterwards. This cove is only affected by big swells when you have Easterly winds.

Approach

To get to Anstey's from Exeter take the A380 sign posted Torquay or from Plymouth come off the A38 onto the A383 and follow this until it meets the A380. From here follow signs to Torquay and join the A379 sign posted Babbacombe. After 2 miles turn right after the Palace Hotel and follow this to the car park. Get changed here and take the track down to the cove.

Entry	Exit	Car Park	Post Code
SX 935 647	SX 935 651	SX 935 645	TQ1 2QP

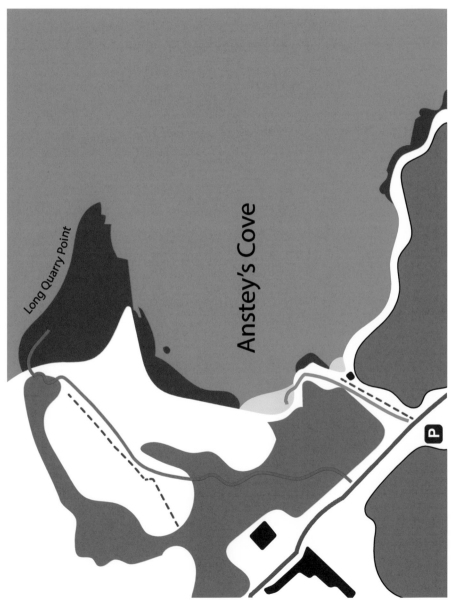

Description

Head left from the café, go over the railings and wade 15m to a small beach. This is where the fun begins. The next 100m consists of large boulders, small jumps and plenty of sumps to explore. When you reach the main cliff face you will come across a small island which has some great jumping spots. The take off's are easy and the sea is deep enough at most states of tide.

Just across from the island there are two jumping platforms with deep landings. To reach the first, climb up 3m on easy holds to an overhanging ledge. The second jump is one of the biggest here, climb up to the left of jump one to a large grass ledge. This jump is 6-8m and a good jumping technique is essential.

To continue, traverse along on great holds for 50m until you reach a large platform with a 7-8m jump from the pinnacle. Do not forget to look out for the seal. He is known as Big Ben to the local fishermen. Over the back of this platform is an impressive zawn which contains some interesting rock formations and a small gully which creates exciting features with any swell. This leads to a large pinnacle and platform called Long Quarry Point. Under the big overhang is a small cave, swim in and climb out to reach the big platform. There is lots of jumping potential from here. The most popular being the 8-10m jump off the overhanging ledge. The landing is deep at most tides although there is a big rock to the right of the landing which must be avoided.

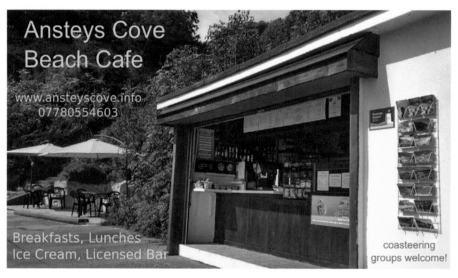

Ansteys Cove
Beach Cafe

www.ansteyscove.info
07780554603

Breakfasts, Lunches
Ice Cream, Licensed Bar

coasteering
groups welcome!

From here you can reach the coastal path via a steep footpath and then follow the road back to the car par. This takes 15-20mins but it is a scenic walk and you can explore more jumps on the way. Alternatively you could return the way you came and enjoy the best parts all over again. When you reach the small island there is a well-used footpath which takes you back to the beach, skipping the boulder field. Why not enjoy a drink or some food at the Anstey's Cove Café afterwards.

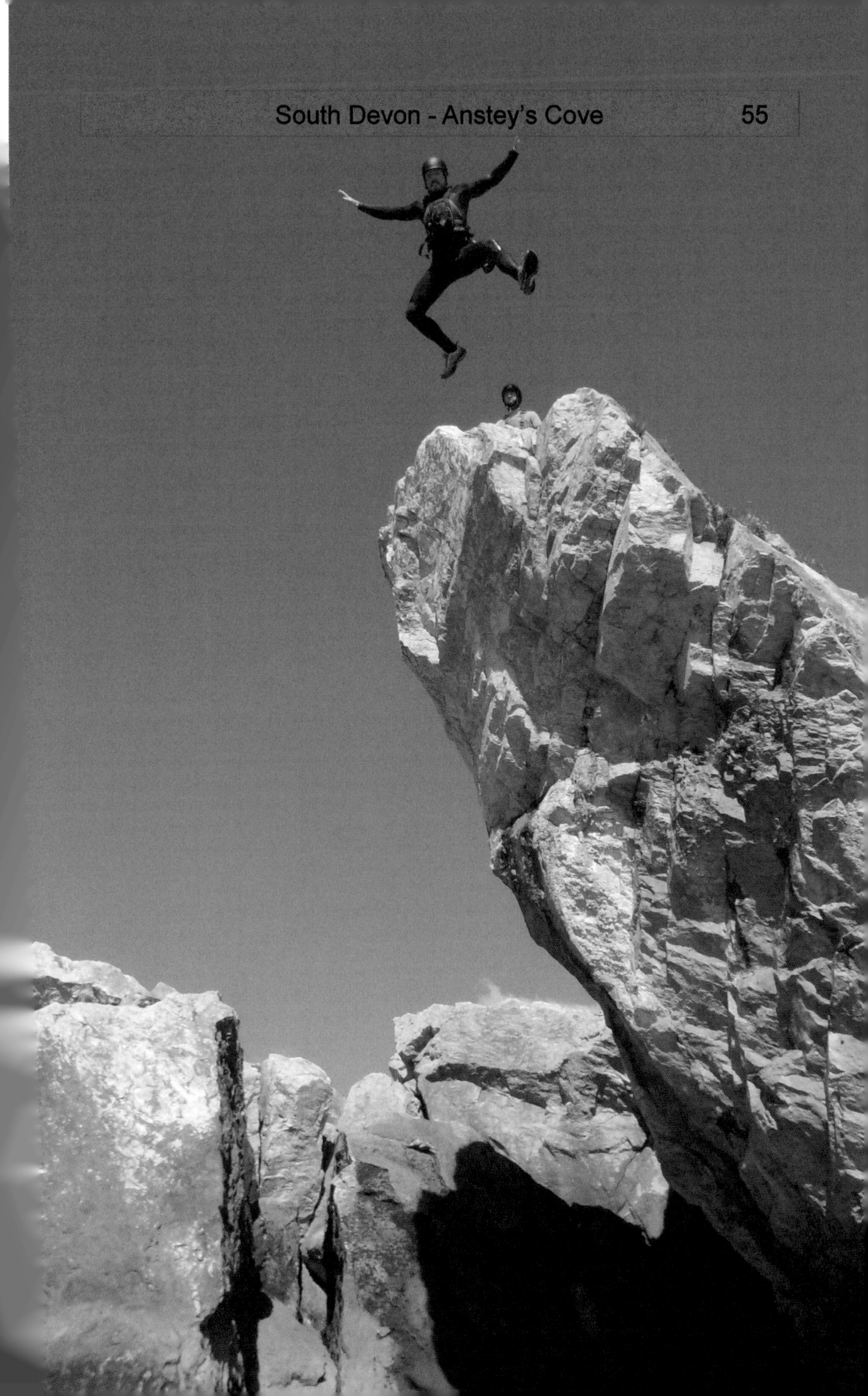

Daddyhole

Torquay is a sea resort town with some outstanding coastline. This trips takes you from Daddyhole to the impressive London Bridge natural arch. Expect calm seas and big jumps with plenty of excellent traversing. The walk in can feel a bit exposed and does require some scrambling.

Approach

Drive into Torquay on the A3022 following signs for the town centre and sea front. When you reach the seafront turn left on the A379. Follow this through the town and around the marina. At the second roundabout turn right onto Victoria road, this leads you around the marina towards the coastline. Keep driving up hill past the Living Coasts and Imperial Hotel then turn right onto Daddyhole Road. Take the next right and the car park is 100m further on. From here walk across the big field towards the Coastguard tower. In front of the tower is a railing and a steep rough track. Follow this all the way down until you scramble into the quarry.

500m	200m	600m				0.5m	18m
Entry	**Exit**		**Car Park**			**Post Code**	
SX 926 627	SX 922 628		SX 926 629			TQ1 2EG	

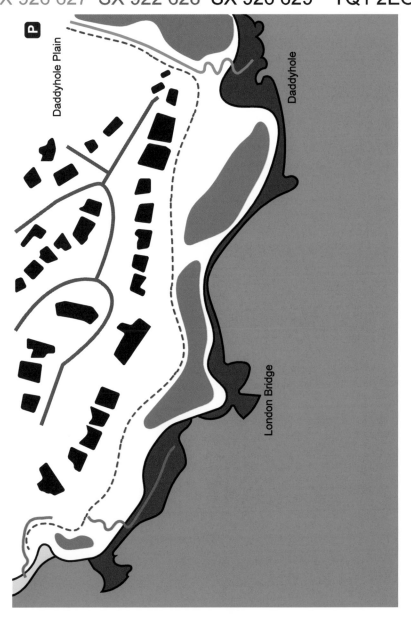

Description

The jumps start straight away. Along the edge of the old quarry are at least 4 jumps of varying heights to start you off. The biggest being a 10-12m jump at the bottom of the decent path. Continue right along some great climbing and more small jumps. The small zawn up ahead is a natural coasteering playground. It has a hard to reach overhanging rock which looks like a diving platform and 7-9m jumps off the opposite side. Around the corner is a big platform which slopes up to an excellent 7m overhanging jump into really deep water. The next 200m is either a long rewarding traverse or a swim. There are jumps to be had along here and some small caves to explore.

The last and best feature is the natural arch known as London Bridge. It's an impressive sight and has some of the best jumps of the trip. Before swimming through the arch climb up to the 10-12m jumps either side. To reach the left hand side jump, climb up the seaward side of the arch. The climb is a long way up on loose rock. The right hand side jump is an easy scramble up to a solid take off. Both jumps require good technique in the air and on landing to avoid injury. Under the arch is a long boulder that blocks any potential jumps from the arch itself. Swim through the arch, look up, and wonder how on earth the arch roof is still there. Jumps ranging from 2-12m litter the left hand side and a short swim then takes you across to the get out. It's not over yet though. Follow the worn track up and you will notice a balancing rock on the cliff edge. The jump off the ledge below the rock is known as Mummy Mac. Daddy Mac is off the rock itself and Granddad Mac is the near suicidal (you have been warned) 15-18m jump above the balancing rock. To escape continue up the track to a low wall. Climb over this and on the right is a set of steps which lead to the path back.

Brixham

Brixham is a small fishing town which has some amazing coastline. The area is popular for climbing, sea kayaking and diving. The coasteering here is great for beginners as it is usually sheltered and the jumps and climbs are very user friendly.

Approach

Brixham can be reached from either Paignton on the A3022 or Dartmouth on the A379. Follow signs for the harbour then turn right onto Berry Head Road. You will pass the Breakwater Bistro on your left, the food here is great and Shoalstone Car Park is 1 minute further on. There is usually plenty of room here and it has a toilet block.

700m	100m	1km	3	0.5m	10m
Entry		Exit	Car Park		Post Code
SX 937 568		SX 944 566	SX 936 567		TQ5 9AH

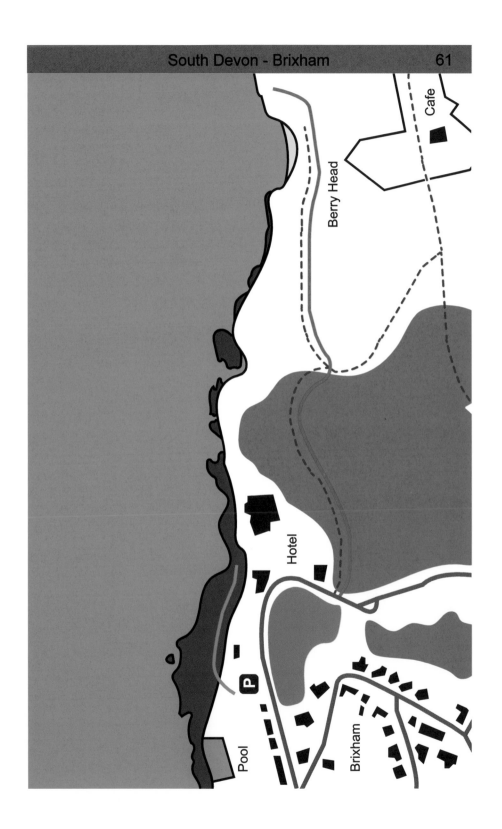

Cafe

Berry Head

Hotel

Pool

P

Brixham

Description

Start by walking out onto the large flat slab which makes up the first 100m. A short swim brings you to the small rock islands where there are plenty of jumps and small climbs. The jumps here are amazing fun, big landing areas and large platforms to launch from. More big flat slabs wait further on. These are slightly higher and the landing areas are not so clean but there is a lot to jump from. Swim 50m onto the next slabs and scramble over to the next features. The cliffs get higher from here and climbing out will be hard and dangerous until you reach the end.

Where the slab joins the cliff it creates a small 4m pool. It is possible to jump from the several ledges above into this pool. Warning, it is a very narrow landing with sloping sides to it. Around the next gully is a 2m sump which is easier to find at low tide. You will see two prominent rock towers. The first is a 4-5m jump with an easy climb up, this warms you up for the next one. The 5-6m jump from the second tower is great for photos and to introduce people to jumping from height. It is overhanging slightly, has a solid take off and a deep landing area. Behind this rock is a small cave which you can swim under. Scramble or swim the next 150m to the old quarry. Climb out just before the concrete wall which at low tides is a 10m climb and can be tricky for the beginner. It's not over yet, jumping off the wall is good safe fun. The old tower here has been jumped off before but only at high tide. You can continue your trip further along the old quarry and head back when your done. This area has some good jumps and small caves to swim through or under depending on the tide. Walk up the tarmac which leads out of the quarry and take the first path right through the woods. Follow this path until you go past the big hotel and hit the road. 100m further on is the car park.

Start Point

Start Point is the most exposed headland on the English coast. It has a lighthouse which in 1836 was used to warn off ships and is now used to broadcast Radio 5. Start Point is a popular spot for walkers and the car park can get quite busy. There is plenty here for the coasteerer; big jumps, tight squeezes and an interesting coastline. Seals are a common sight here.

Approach

Approach from Kingsbridge or Slapton on the A379. Drive to the village of Stokenham and at the roundabout take the road signposted Prawle and Beesands. You pick up signs for Start Point shortly after. Follow this winding country road for 6km to the car park. To get to the beach take the large muddy track at the southern end of the car park.

Entry	Exit	Car Park	Post Code
SX 817 369	SX 825 370	SX 821 375	TQ7 2ET

Lighthouse

Start Point

To The Car Park

Description

The first 300m is made up of flat rock slabs with shallow gullies and one 5m overhanging jump. It is possible to skip round to the cave via the path if you are short on time or if the swell is making the first section difficult. Where the small track finishes you come to a sheltered area which has an entry jump and an intimidating cave. The sea can be very murky here if there is any swell and judging the depth is difficult - watch out for hidden fins of rock. The cave is brilliant, you can swim through a small gap to reach the shingle beach at the back of it.

Small jumps and easy scrambling keep your interest as you move over the next 100m. Look down the long zawn and up to your left are a series of big jumps. From here swim 50m across the bay until you reach a large chunk of rock and one of the best jumps here. It's between 8-10m depending on tide and can be reached by easy climbing on either side. Behind this rock is a narrow 20m channel to squeeze through. It is possible to scramble out here back to the main path SX 821 368. If you continue the small inlet has small jumps and short swims between the islands.

It's 350m until the next exit point. There is little of interest here but it does give you an extended trip. The exit point is steep and dangerous in wet conditions SX 825 370. It is possible to get in here and explore the area between here and the lighthouse. The islands have some good 8-10m jumps and there are some great caves to delve into, including the spider grotto. This cave has a big entrance which shrinks quickly to a spider filled vertical exit. Unfortunately this area is less sheltered and there are no exit points until you reach the privately owned lighthouse. Beware this extension is a serious undertaking with strong rips, not a section for the inexperienced.

Starehole Bay

Starehole Bay is a sheltered bay just South of Salcombe. The route takes you along the south side of the bay along the side of Bolt Head. The trip has jumps, climbs and some interesting rock formations. The walk in gives you a preview of the stunning scenery in the area. At high tide you will get bigger and better jumps but some of the best features will be under water. At low tide you get the best all round experience.

Approach

Follow the A381 towards Salcombe until your reach the village of Malborough. Turn off at the Texaco garage and follow signs to Soar. Just before the village the road forks, right is sign posted Soar Mill Hotel, take the left fork. ½ a mile further on you will come to a big car park. Walk from here to East Soar Farm or to Bolt Head and take one of the many footpaths leading down to Starehole Bay. These paths are well posted but if in doubt head down. The access to the beach has seen some landslides so take care. When you reach the bay the walk in seems well worth it.

Entry	Exit	Car Park	Post Code
SX 726 365	SX 723 360	SX 712 375	TQ7 3DS

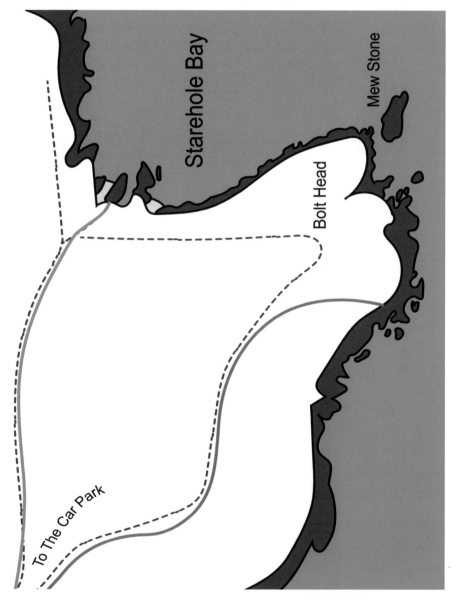

Description

Carefully climb down the makeshift steps into the sea. Walk out onto the beach and head right for the first rocks you see. The beach is separated by a spit of land which has two caves that go all the way through. You can swim through these at high water. Scramble over the jumble of rocks to the first small jumps, easily accessible and fun for all. The next 100m is scrambling and rock hopping and then you reach a rock tower. Climb the back of the tower to reach the good 6-8m jumps - these are only deep enough at high tide.

Continue along, traversing and making the most out of the small jumping ledges. The next big feature is a deep 40m channel created by a small island. The jumps here are numerous and the narrow landings make them a challenge. Another 150m of excellent traversing brings you opposite the Mew stone, a large island usually covered in birds. 200m of small islands, gullies and short swims bring you to the blue lagoon. This feature is best at low tide, a series of rocks form a deep 10m pool surrounded by jumps. Once you have finished it's a slog back up the hill to reach the coastal path back.

Hope Cove

Hope Cove is a small fishing village made up of two parts, Inner Hope and Outer Hope. The trip takes you from the cove and along the cliffs of the Bolt Tail, an impressive headland that sticks out into Bigbury Bay. I have often seen friendly seals here which are a bonus to the journey. Bolt Tail should only be explored in calm conditions. The cliffs are imposing and the route finding is challenging. A great venue for the experienced coasteerer.

Approach

Drive down the A381 towards Salcombe and take the well signposted turn off, 3 miles from Salcombe, for Hope Cove. The cove is 2 miles further on. As you descend the hill turn left following signs for the Inner Hope. Park opposite the hotel. From here follow signs for the coastal path and walk up the steps to reach the top of the headland.

900m 900m 1.3km

Entry **Exit** **Car Park** **Post Code**

SX 669 398 SX 668 397 SX 676 397 TQ7 3HN

0.5m 10m

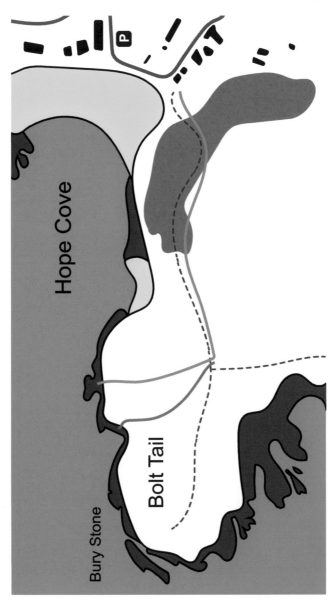

Hope Cove

Bolt Tail

Bury Stone

Description

After the walk up the hill make your way down to the cliffs by following small tracks. There are two spits of rock that jut out, climb down the one closest to the beach to begin. This can be difficult to find so be patient. Start heading out towards the headland by scrambling between the small islands. As you enter the first bay a large cave greets you. This cave goes back a good 40m and is often home to seals.

Continue along making the most out of the small jumps until you reach an island separated by narrow gullies. The main gully is fun to jump into and getting washed around in here is exciting. This is also your exit point, follow the narrow ridge of rock up to the path. Do not get out yet, the best is yet to come. The next feature is the Bury Stone, a large island off of the headland. Any swell is magnified in this area - only carry on exploring in calm conditions. Climb up onto the Bury Stone where there are two wave shaped rocks to jump from. The first is only possible at high tide but the second one will go at lower tides. The landings are not completely clear, there are large boulders under the water and you will need a clear flat day to spot these the first time round. The sea rushes through this gap so ensure you take the time to read the water before entering. There are no escape routes further around the headland but there is a huge amount to explore. Keep in mind that you will have to double back as you continue around the Bolt Tail. The cliffs tower over you as you get to the next bay and the 8m jump into a narrow gully is intimidating as you have to clear the ledges below. The bay has lots to offer, more caves to delve into and a series of scrambles. I suggest you head back from here because of the exposed headland and the lack of exit points, this would be a bad place to have any kind of issue.

North Devon

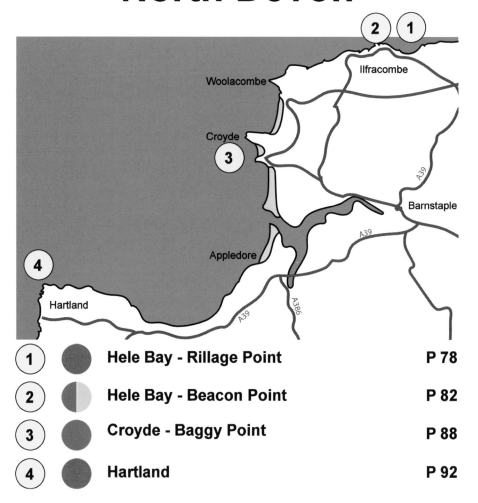

1		**Hele Bay - Rillage Point**	**P 78**
2		**Hele Bay - Beacon Point**	**P 82**
3		**Croyde - Baggy Point**	**P 88**
4		**Hartland**	**P 92**

The majority of the coastline between Minehead in Somerset and Hartland in North Devon is made up of long shallow beaches and huge inaccessible cliffs. Fortunately between these features are some amazing coves and headlands to coasteer around. Large slate slabs and fins create most of the features in the area and there is always a sheltered cove to coasteer in when the seas are bigger. The following guides are the best locations in the area.

Hele Bay - Rillage Point

The trip from Hele Bay to the coastguard cottages is fantastic but it comes with some risks. The shallow sloping sea bed causes any swell to jack up magnifying the power of the sea and the gullies have strong tidal flows that rip through them. The trip is also very exposed. You are surrounded by high cliffs and very few escape routes. I recommend going on a flat day to get to know the trip and then trying it with more swell if you're confident. Many of the beach sections get cut off at high tide, so I recommend approaching this section on a dropping tide.

Approach

Hele Bay is located between Ilfracombe and Combe Martin on the A399. From either direction it is well signposted. Turn down to the bay by the Hele Bay Pub - a good place for a pint afterwards and then park in the big Pay and Display car park. The beach has toilets and a café.

Entry	Exit	Car Park	Post Code
SS 536 479	SS 544 485	SS 536 477	EX34 9QZ

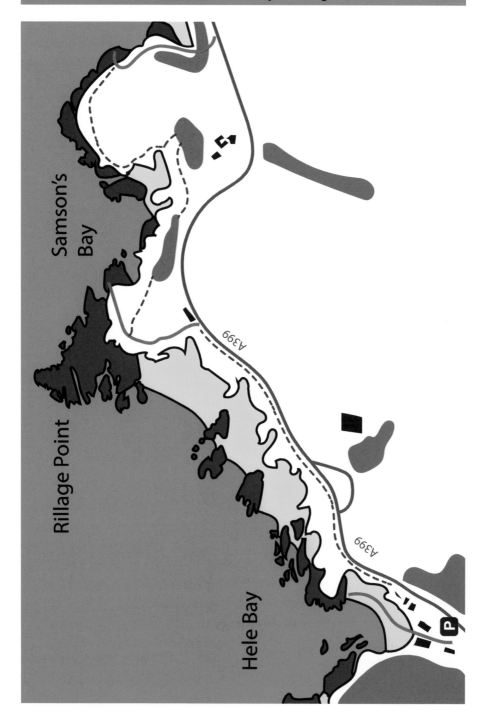

Samson's Bay

Rillage Point

Hele Bay

A399

A399

Description

The first fins of rock create some small but interesting gullies which give you an indication of what is to come. If you find crossing these difficult then head back and go around Beacon Point. As you climb around the corner there are a multitude of jumps and mini islands to investigate. The biggest is an 8m jump from a large grassy topped slab. Beware the lose rocks that litter the take off. This area gets shallow quickly so a good inspection of the landing is needed.

Swim or traverse to the beach. At lower tides you can walk most of the way along the 300m beach and there are a few interesting caves along the way. As you move into the spit of rocks you catch a glimpse of Rillage Point through the narrow slots. There are two large scoops worn out of the rock up ahead. The sea washes in through one and fills the other. It's lots of fun to ride the waves in between them. From here make your way to the point. Scramble and swim between gullies heading clockwise around the point. You then you reach a large slot gap which separates the end of the point from the mainland.

The jumps here are big although the slot gets shallow quickly and exaggerates any swell. The sea can rush through here creating dangerous conditions, go in with caution at all times. Once you have exhausted the slot make your way around the rest of the point. You will pass through several canyon like gullies before reaching the small beach.

From here you can traverse out of the bay all the way to the end of the trip. It's not over yet though. Look out for the large slab which at some point has been used as a slip way, there is still concrete covering some of it. Here are the last jumps of the trip. The highest being around 10m. Exit here up the path that wiggles up and through the undergrowth. In the summer it can be hard to find but once you are above the cliff keep heading west and up until you reach the coastal path up to the cottages. The path then continues down into Hele following the A379. To extend your trip carry on around Samson's Bay to the next headland. The bay has a great sea arch to swim through and the gully crossings can be exciting. Towards the end of the bay is a large slab with 3 jumps ranging from 3m - 6m. You can scramble up from here or carry on until you reach the entrance of Watermouth Cove, where there is a thin track which leads to the coastal path and the road.

Hele Bay - Beacon Point

Hele Bay is a sheltered beach East of Ilfracombe. Due to the two headlands guarding the bay it is often protected from rough conditions. This section describes the route heading West and it is used regularly by coasteering providers. At high tide expect to do some swimming between the islands to get to the jumps. At lower tides interesting gullies form but the depth is harder to judge.

Approach

Hele Bay is located between Ilfracombe and Combe Martin on the A399. From either direction it is well signposted. Turn down to the bay by the Hele Bay Pub, a good place for a pint afterwards and then park in the big pay and display car park. The beach has toilets and a café.

Entry	Exit	Car Park	Post Code
SS 536 479	SS 529 477	SS 536 477	EX34 9QZ

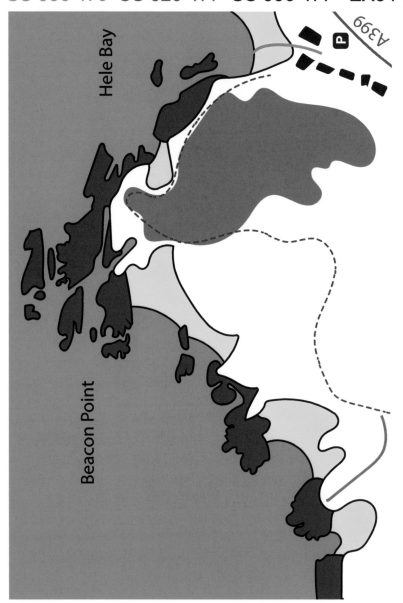

Description

®SoggyLemming

From the sandy beach head left and follow the cliff westwards. There is a dry route here via a small scramble around the back of the first rock outcrops. There are small ribs of rock to climb over along this section which break up the journey to the small bay. The bay is dominated by a large slab of rock with a sloping face. At high tide the base of this slab can be jumped off but beware the sunken rock which guards the higher jumps. Swim or scramble around to the fantastic rock arch and beach which are ideal for a quick picture. From here you can see the islands that compose the majority of the trip. Explore the gullies and islands making sure you test the depths thoroughly before jumping. There is far too much here to describe it all and in even small swell you can find really fun features to play in. As the islands push out to sea you will find a large one which is easy to climb onto and has jumps of up to 7m depending on the tides. Enjoy the last few outcrops of this section making sure to play in the pour overs.

This is the end of the beginner route so head back to Hele trying an alternate route through the gullies. If you decide to continue on the intermediate route to Rapparee Cove then make your way into the small bay with a beach and start to follow the cliffs along. There are no escape routes until you get to the cove and the depths are hard to judge, I recommend doing this route at low tide first to give you a glimpse of the sea bed and warn you of any hidden obstacles. Come back at high tide to really enjoy this section.

As you follow the cliffs along you will see the two rock arches which are the highlights of the trip. The first has a large bowl like base where the sea has worn its way into the cliffs. Go past this and scramble up to the large slab which ends above the bowl. From here you can see Ilfracombe through the large arches. At spring high tide you can jump or flop into the hole and if there is any swell you will get washed around and sucked out to sea - extremely fun. Moving on you will see the next rock arch, swim or climb through it to find a small cove with a large island. As you exit the archway look right into the narrow gully which leads out to sea. There are jumps from both sides and getting sucked out into the wider section is as fun as the jumps. Swim back through to the back of the cove and around the small island where you will see a body sized hole. You can spend ages here, getting washed through the hole at a rapid rate and then getting sucked back through again. Beware an undercut rock on the right hand side. Once you have exhausted this, move through another narrow slot and around onto a small headland. There are a few pool like areas here. Some are deep enough to jump into and the swell recirculates you around them like an emptying sink. Unfortunately this is the end of the adventure. Scramble round to the beach then head up the stairs which lead to the main road and back. You could follow the coastal path back which will give you little glimpses of the route you have just done.

®SoggyLemming

Croyde - Baggy Point

Croyde is one of North Devon's best surfing beaches, it is also ideal for coasteering. Many providers use this venue, so expect to see groups out and about. There are numerous entry and exit points giving you options to shorten or lengthen your trip. The narrow gullies and ribs are extremely fun for all abilities.

Approach

Croyde can be reached from either Ilfracombe or Barnstaple on the A361. Drive to Braunton then take the Saunton road to Croyde. Follow signs for Baggy Point and Croyde beach. The National Trust car park is near the end of the road. Walk up the road past the café. There is an entry point opposite the last house if you fancy 100m of rock hopping and gully exploration. The next entry point is 200m further on, just as the path turns right.

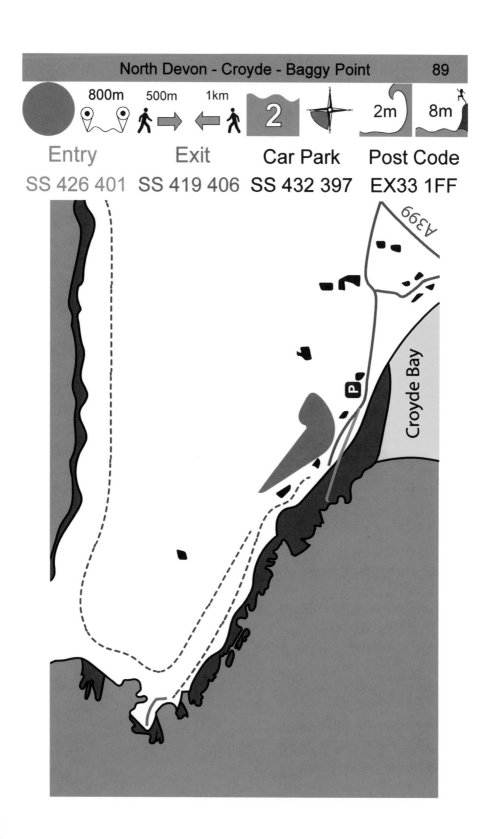

800m   500m   1km   2   2m   8m

Entry   **Exit**   **Car Park**   **Post Code**

SS 426 401   SS 419 406   SS 432 397   EX33 1FF

A399

Croyde Bay

P

Description

This section consists of lots of narrow channels and every time you go, you find a new one to explore. The water depth is hard to judge because of the murky conditions and sneaky fins of rock await the unwary. Even in big swell these channels can be quite sheltered allowing you to pop in and out of the rougher areas.

The first channels hold many of the jumps and most of the landing areas are narrow but deep enough towards high tide. As you progress, the channels get shallow which causes the swell to push through and create some fun play spots. Every so often it opens out and exposes you to the swell - good timing is necessary to avoid splatting the sides. Choose your own path, balancing over the knife edge fins and progressing through the maze of gullies until you get to the large bay. As the bay opens out you will see a large cave with an alluring ledge 10m up on the left hand side. This can be accessed by the long slab next to the cave. This jump is only possible at high tide due to the shallow bed of the cave entrance. If in doubt leave it for another day.

Cross the bay towards the cave entrance embedded in the side of the headland. This cave is 50m long and goes under the headland itself. At the cave entrance is a bowl like pool which is deep enough to jump into from the ledges above the cave. This gets shallow quick and the bowl can contain rock debris so check thoroughly before jumping. At high tide the cave becomes flooded and traps fish and unwary explorers in it, allow yourself plenty of time to get through it. The swell can rush through here creating weird water features in the cave mouth and it fills fast as you approach high tide. Exit the cave and scramble up the slab to the top of the headland and back to the footpath. If the cave is full you can climb up various ways to get back.

Hartland Quay

Photo by happyhiker.co.uk

Hartland Quay is a popular starting point for walkers on the coastal path and because of this it has lots of parking and a great pub. The coasteering here is a mix between extreme rock pooling, a romantic walk on the beach, and fear. The escape routes are few and far between and the surrounding cliffs are full of loose rock. It is still a fun adventure though and the rock formations add to the scenic nature of the trip.

Approach

Drive on the A39 from either Bideford or Bude. Turn off on the B3248 signposted Hartland, its 2 miles to the village. Hartland quay is well signposted, follow the winding road until you reach the quay. Parking at the top gives you easy access to the coastal path but there is also parking available around the back of the pub.

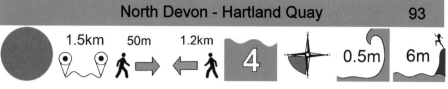

Entry	Exit	Car Park	Post Code
SS 222 247	SS 225 236	SS 222 247	EX39 6DU

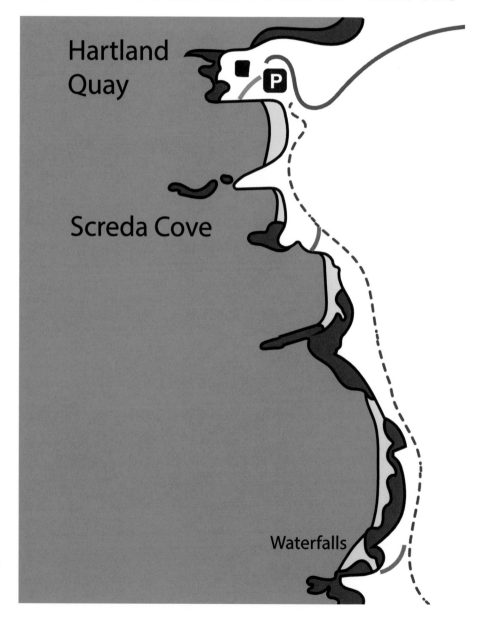

Hartland Quay

Screda Cove

Waterfalls

Description

If the conditions look big from the car park then save this trip for another day. There is only one escape route or alternate entry on this section, the rope descent at SS 225 243. Access to the sea is over the car park wall and down the rib of rock. In swell the swim to the first island is a good test to decide if you carry on or not. There are numerous jumps from the rib and the island and then an 80m swim takes you onto the big beach where all sorts of debris is washed up.

Walk along the beach to start of Screda Point. The point is broken up into a few islands which are separated by small channels. In swell waves hit the point and speed up along the sides making it difficult to swim and scramble around it. Use the first channel to cut around most of the point. Some tricky climbing rewards you with a 6m jump and an 80m swim to the next beach. Climb around the next point. This is Childspit Beach, as you reach the beach look left and you will see a 4m slab. You can climb this slab to reach the path out or alternately start here. Walk along the beach, exploring the washed up treasures until you reach the next point. This huge slab of rock has some really good rock pools. Some of which are deep enough to jump into and some of the jumps can reach 4m. These rock pools continue along until the next beach and are ideal for hunting down sea creatures. As you head in towards the next beach there is a natural sea cave to crawl through to access the long beach. You have to earn the next bit of excitement by walking 400m along the beach. You can exit via the steps or continue around the spit to a series of fresh water falls which are deep with two good jumping ledges. Scramble up to the coastal path and walk back to the cars to finish.

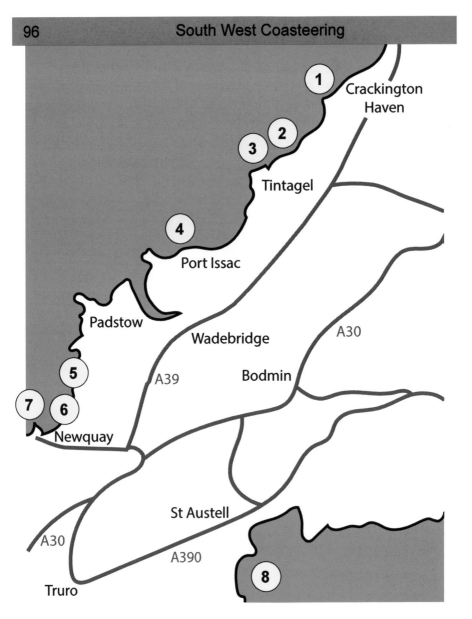

This section of Cornwall is a coasteering Mecca, with lots of venues within a short drive. The venues differ vastly in character - you have hard to reach islands surrounded by 70m cliffs and small coves full of caves and jumps. The venues are well placed to combine your coasteering with surfing, climbing, sea kayaking and sightseeing. The following guides are a selection of the coasteering in the area.

East Cornwall

Crackington Haven

Crackington Haven is a beautiful spot which is very popular with surfers. It has convenient parking and a great pub for after your trip. At high tide this trip involves more swimming and the only feature that stands out is the final jump known as Gonads. There is also a very strong rip off the beach so take note of the signs. At lower tides, more features become exposed and there is more to do, although the end jump may not be deep enough. You want calm conditions here as the headland can get pounded by swell.

Approach

Get to Crackington via the A39 from Bude or Wadebrige direction. Turn off at either Wainhouse Corner or down the B3263. Crackington is well signposted and the car park is just off the beach by the Pub. From the car park cross the road and start scrambling over the rocks on the north side off the beach.

Entry	Exit	Car Park	Post Code
SX142 969	SX 139 973	SX143 967	EX23 0JG

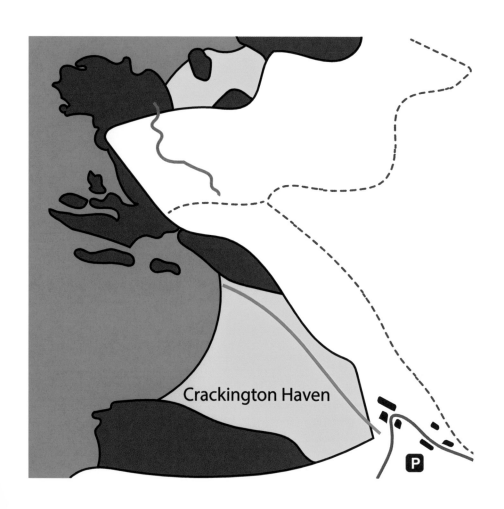

Crackington Haven

Description

The first 200m consists of rock hopping over big boulders or a swim at high tide. The cliffs overhead are very lose and rock fall is a common occurrence. The real fun begins when you reach the first of a series of rock spits. Although the jumps are not massive, swimming and scrambling through the gullies is great fun. There are jumps between the first rock islands but keep an eye on the depth and watch out for fins of rock hiding just under the water.

The first islands join near the cliff to form a rounded dead end. The rock formations here are cool and a small swell can wash around here creating features to play in. After you have had enough of the rock fins and islands, move on toward a big imposing slab. You can scramble up to the wide ledge at the top where the biggest jump takes off from. It gets shallow quickly here and the top jump only works at higher tides. If the depth is not there for the top jump, then climb down and traverse under the slab and you will find several small jumping ledges that work at most tides. Explore the headland where seals are a common sight and narrow trenches create some fun play spots. To finish either head back the way you came or scramble up to the steep ridge and onto the coastal path which leads back to the car park.

Saddle Rocks

Saddle Rocks are a jumble of rock islands that stick out from the cliffs between Rocky Valley and Boscastle. This venue is exposed and hard to reach but it feels like a real adventure. The islands are popular with wildlife so expect some close seal encounters. Even a small swell makes this a dangerous place, strong currents push through and around the islands causing difficult and unpredictable conditions. If you have nice flat conditions get in at Bossiney Haven and coasteer all the way to Saddle Rocks. It's an amazing day out with a huge amount to explore. Get outs are very limited and it is a tiring trip so it may not be for everyone.

Approach

From the A39 take the B3314 signposted Tintagel and Boscastle. Follow signs to Tintagel and drive through the village to Bossiney. Carry on through Bossiney and Rocky Valley is just under a 1km further on. There is a large lay by to park in. Cross the road and follow signposts for the coastal path. This leads you down into to scenic valley through the woods and an old ruin. The ruin is home to a carved labyrinth believed to date back to the Bronze Age. Once you reach the gorge go over the footbridge and follow the path up the steep hill. Follow the coastal path until you reach a wooden stile. The stone wall is now on your right. Walk along it for 150m and you will see the very faint track down to the sea. This track is extremely slippery when wet, if it's raining maybe think about a different venue. Zigzag down the grassy slope until it turns to rock. Descend down this to sea.

Entry	Exit	Car Park	Post Code
SX 074 902	SX 074 902	SX 073 890	PL34 0BB

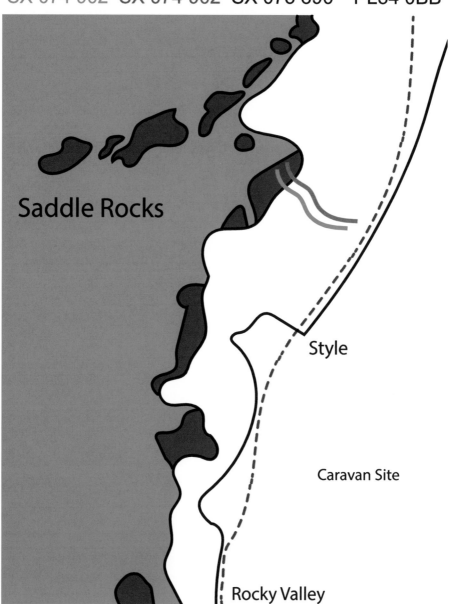

Saddle Rocks

Style

Caravan Site

Rocky Valley

Description

After braving the descent path it is a relief to get into the sea. As you look out you will see the small islands that make up the route. Directly ahead there is a conical shaped island with a small channel running between it and the huge cliff face. As you swim through the gap the sense of exposure increases. The first main island has some easy climbing on its face and a series of jumps at different heights. Jumping from the top of the island is about 10m and requires a big jump out to clear the slab below.

It's only a short swim to the next island which is joined with a second island by a narrow zawn. In the zawn there are 6m jumps from either side into a small 2m landing area. The sides slope down and join making it shallower the deeper you go.. The next 50m has extensive climbing along it and another short swim brings you to the final island. Again this island has plenty of good climbing for all ability levels and a 5m jumping ledge which runs along the length of it. Explore the other sides of the islands and return to the starting slab. There is lots more to explore here, 100m west of the decent path is a series of ledges over deep water. These jumps go as high as 15m and are a great finish to the trip.

Bossiney Haven

Bossiney Haven is a popular beach for dog walkers and surfers. At low tide you can walk out on the amazing sandy beach but as the tide starts to come in, it becomes a great coasteering venue. If you have flat conditions you can continue your trip to Rocky Valley SX071896 or all the way to Saddle Rocks P95.

Approach

Coming from either direction on the A39, turn off on the B3314 towards Tintagel and Boscastle. After Slaughterbridge take the B3263 turn off towards Tintagel. Drive through Tintagel, admiring the many pasty shops and 2 miles later you will reach Bossiney. The car park is 100m past the Ocean Cove Holiday Park on your left. The car park has a voluntary payment box and toilets. Once changed go through the gate and follow the footpath down to the cove.

Entry	Exit	Car Park	Post Code
SX 066 893	SX 066 893	SX 067 889	PL34 0AY

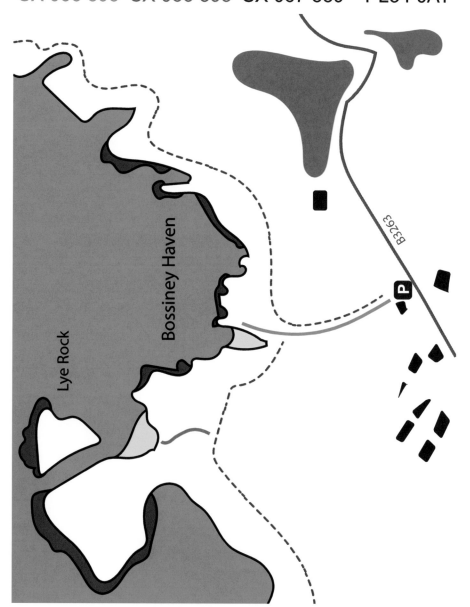

Description

On first sight, the cove is impressive and on a still day it is quiet and secluded. One hour either side of high tide the sea comes into the narrow entrance. This can cause some issues if there is a strong Westerly or Northerly swell. As the cove entrance narrows the swell heightens and breaks onto shallow water causing a strong rip. Swimming through this can be tricky and tiring.

Swim or walk, depending on the tide through the stunning rock arch and into a huge cave. The cave goes back about 30m and soon gets pitch black - beware of sea creatures. For the next 100m continue scrambling and swimming, keeping the cliffs on your left. Across the bay you will find some fun caves to explore and at high tide there are jumps here. You will soon come to a series of jumps from big rock ledges. There are many jumping options from these ledges and some great climbs up to them. The top ledge has seen many people back off due to its tight landing area between the sloping slabs.

Continue round until you get to a small rocky bay. There is a winding fishing track here which can be used to escape back to the car park. In the summer it can become very overgrown and hard to spot. Either scramble along the beach here or swim across to the big zawn. This zawn separates Lye Rock from the headland. Beware the zawn is prone to rock fall. Being in here makes you feel tiny and a bit exposed but towards the back of the zawn are some exciting 6-10m jumps. As you exit the zawn continue round to the right for 50m. Here there is a small inlet with an 8m jump on the left hand side. Turn back here and return through the zawn. Either go back the way you came or use the fishing track and walk back to the car park. As mentioned before the swim back into the cove can be difficult due to the shallow beach and breaking waves, so if your team is feeling tired, the fishing track is a sensible option.

Port Gaverne

Port Gaverne is a small but very busy fishing village. During the summer holidays this village is heaving and with very little parking it can be tricky to find a spot. It's worth it though, as the coasteering is exciting and full of amazing caves.

Approach

Coming from either direction on the A39 turn off on the B3314 towards Tintagel and Port Issac. About 8 miles down the road turn off on the B3267 signposted Port Gaverne and Port Issac. Port Gaverne is 2.5 miles further on and is well signposted. The car park is up the hill on the left of the beach as you look out to sea.

Entry	Exit	Car Park	Post Code
SX 002 809	SX 002 809	SW 999 810	PL29 3SB

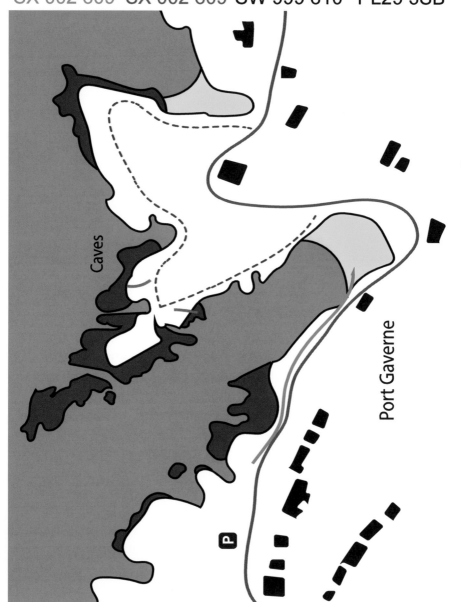

Description

From the beach, either swim along the right hand side of the cliffs or walk up onto the headland and follow the path to the small steps into the sea. Easy rock hopping brings you to the obvious gap separating an island of rock from the headland. As the swell washes through here, it increases in size and can break. This is great fun or really scary depending on your point of view. The big ledge that runs along the gap is a solid launching platform for some 3-5m jumps. Good timing is essential if the swell is pushing through here. If these are not big enough for you or you're trying to impress someone, look up and you will see another ledge which is pretty much the top of the headland. The climb up is a scary enough experience in its own right but when you reach the top you find a stable platform and a 9-12m jump (tide depending).

Exit the gap from either end and explore the island of rock sticking out into the sea. This little outcrop has plenty of jumps ranging from 3-5m in height. At mid tide with a swell running, you get a cauldron of water which washes you around and around. Head back past the gap and along the East side of the headland where there are a series of inlets which all have caves at the back. The first cave goes back 50m, then goes pitch black. Don't be put off. Feel your way onwards and you will see a thin crack of light to your left. At low tide it is possible to get all the way through. The next entrance leads to a block choked cave. This cave goes all the way through to a stunning bay with a loud blow hole in certain conditions. Scramble your way back round to the cave entrance and start the journey back. Either go all the way back to the steps or climb out on one of the easy climbs before the island.

Porth Island

Porth Island juts out from Porth, just north of Newquay. It is popular for surfing, coasteering and holiday makers. The coasteering is great, it has caves to explore and jumps to test your mettle. The trip changes character with the tides. At high water, there can be a lot of swimming and some of the caves will be submerged, although it opens up more jumping opportunities. At low water, the trip is shorter as you can walk/ scramble into and out of the good sections. The jumps that are still deep get very big and you can go all the way through the blow hole cave.

Approach

From the A30 come off at the Indian Queens junction and onto the A39. Follow this onto the A392 which leads to Newquay. When you reach the Quintrell Downs roundabout, turn right following signs to St Columb Minor. Turn left at the T Junction onto the A3059 and shortly after take a right turn signposted for Porth. This leads you to the beach and the car park is on your left opposite the big sandy beach.

Entry / Exit
SW 829 628

Car Park
SW 832 629

Post Code
TR7 3NB

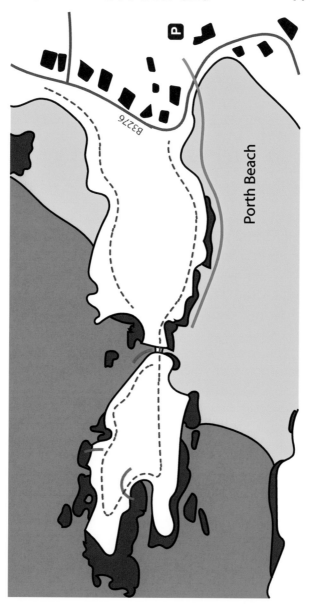

Description

If you are on high tide, then you can access the footpath just up the hill from the car park. This goes all the way to the headland. When you reach a small bridge you can turn left and scramble down to the sea. From here you can swim/traverse to the start of the headland. At low tide, you can walk most of this along the sand. As you get close to the start of the headland, rock islands appear and this is where the trip starts proper.

The caves start straight away and at low tide you can swim into them. At certain times of year the roofs are covered in big mussels, ideal for a free lunch. Move around the mini headland into a large zawn which ends in a sandy beach. Across the zawn is a small hole and crack - this is the blow hole. There is an alternate entry/exit point here. Scramble up next to the blow hole to get onto the footpath. At higher tides with a swell running, air gets pushed out causing a great blow hole. At lower tides you can crawl through it and into the big cave. It's an eerie experience and seals are often seen in here.

As you look out of the cave mouth you will see a series of jumping ledges on the left. Swim along and find a climb up that suits. The jumps range from 6-10m at low tide and the cave mouth is super deep. The next 100m is a traverse or swim. There are jumps along here which are worth a climb up to. The next zawn is the gem of the trip. It is a deep narrow slot which leads into a long ago collapsed cave. The big rock arch above has a small post box hole above it, just big enough to crawl through and jump from. Look down the zawn and a series of ledges on your right give you access to the post box. Sitting on the edge with your feet dangling over is a bit nerve racking and the zawn seems really narrow. You can put a foot on a small ledge which gives you a pretty solid take off point then drop the 8-10m into the slot. Accuracy is key here. The rest of the trip is made up of small juts of rock and swimming. Towards the end of the journey you will find another rock arch. There are jumps from above here at high water and you can also exit back to the footpath here. Swim or walk back to the bridge and go under it. You are now back at the start. Either walk back up the beach or scramble out up to the headland path.

Towan Head

The Gazzle is the east side of Towan Head, which juts out from Newquay. The close proximity to the Cornish Ibiza makes this a popular venue for many coasteering providers. An out of season trip is recommended to avoid the crowds of hen and stag do's. The road runs parallel to the cliffs making scouting easy to do and gives you plenty of exit options. There is a bird nesting site in certain areas of the cove. Please stick to the recommended route and check locally for up to date information.

Approach

The easiest approach is to drive into Newquay on the A392 which ends at the Mount Wise Roundabout. Go straight ahead at the roundabout onto Tower Road. This is signposted Fistral Beach and Newquay Golf Club. Continue to the next roundabout and take the second exit, past the Red Lion Inn on your right. Another 100m further take the left turn, signposted Fistral and Little Fistral. When the road forks, go right towards Towan Head and drive all the way along to the car park at the end. There is parking all along the road.

Entry	Exit	Car Park	Post Code
SW 800 628	SW 802 625	SW 800 627	TR7 1HS

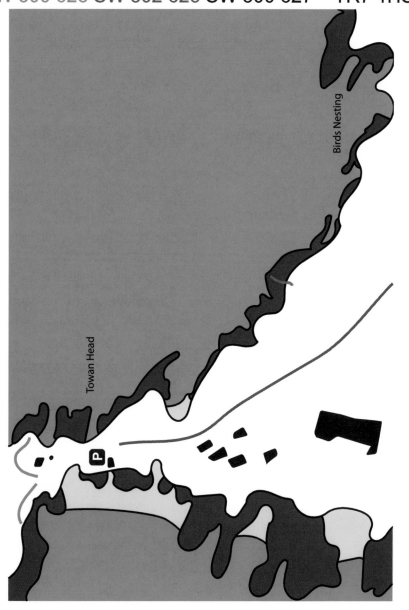

Description

Although there are many entry points along the coastline I recommend getting in near the toilet block or to go around the entire headland and enter via the sandy beach to the West. Between the toilet block and the old lifeboat slipway there are plenty of jumps to get you going. A 3m jump just before the slipway makes a good alternative start. Traverse along bulges of rock with plenty of jumps until you get to the small beach which has a narrow cave set into it. You can traverse out off the beach and along to the next corner.

Climb up here to a fun 4m jump and then swim across to the fantastic triple jump section. The long slab has at least 3 solid jumping points. At higher tide you can jump from the grassy ledge by the track. The landing area is quite narrow and at lower tides you will start to see the protruding ledge opposite. This is a good point to exit or for observers to take photos. In the busy months you can expect to queue up here. The jumps continue along the next section of ledges before you swim into a gully. There is a lot to do here before climbing up the face at the end of the gully to do a final big jump. It is best to head back here even though the caves opposite are very inviting. Above the caves is a bird nesting area. If in doubt check locally for more information. The track by the triple jump leads to the road back to the cars.

Pentire

East Pentire Point is home to the swanky Lewinnick Lodge. It is only a short drive/walk from Newquay and the coasteering is short but packed with activity. At low water it is interesting to walk through the caves and see the shape of the sea bed. It gives you an idea of the water depth you need for the bigger jumps. The best all round experience comes at around high tide. All the islands and gullies give you some shelter during rough conditions, although the narrow constrictions can beef it up.

Approach

The easiest approach is to drive into Newquay on the A392 which ends at the Mount Wise Roundabout. Turn left onto Pentire Road which turns into Pentire Ave. Continue on this road, past the many hotels until you get to the pay and display car park at the end. From the car park, walk up the big footpath towards the headland and follow this until you can turn left to meet the cliff edge. An easy scramble down gives you lots of potential starting points along here. To make sure you do not miss anything start as near to the beach as you can.

800m   300m   800m

Entry   Exit   Car Park   Post Code
SW 785 613 SW 780 616 SW 788 614   TR7 1QD

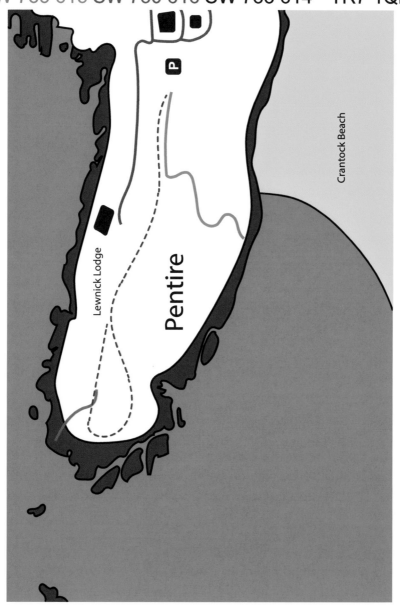

Crantock Beach

Lewnick Lodge

Pentire

Description

The first 100m seems a bit flat as you scramble along broken ledges. It also doesn't look like there is much ahead. Do not worry, it is there, hidden behind the small islands and gullies. The first gully you find is narrow and shallow. This widens up towards the end and there are some small jumps to get you started. In swell the waves pump through but when you have had enough it is easy to climb out and scramble round. Walk over the slab to the wide bay. Looking across the bay you will see a small island 10m from the main cliff and in the back of the bay you will see a dark hole. This hole is the entrance to the cave that runs through a large portion of the coastline. I think it is better to return this way but the option to enter and proceed through the cave now is there. Swim over to the island and make the most of the small jumps off of it. Afterwards climb around the main slab and a cauldron like pool, to enter the start of a narrow gully. In swell, the sea pushes into the cauldron creating some exciting features to play in. If the swell is pushing hard from the cauldron into the gully it is best to avoid getting in.

You can follow the gully or traverse over the slab to get to the main cave area. Here you will see the big cave mouth which leads back to the bay and a long slot that leads to the sea. The slot is created by three islands which all have jumps on. The first island is accessed by a slippery climb up and there are various heights to jump from, all of which have landings in front of the cave, the biggest being an awkward point of rock. Above the cave you will find the biggest and best jumps here. Climb up the slab to get there - it gets very slippery when wet. The water gets shallow quick, so ensure you are here around high water. You get a real free fall feeling off of the top jump - amazing. Follow the slot along to the final island where there is a 4 -6m jump into a very narrow landing. You can climb out here and scramble up to the headland where the path leads back to the car park. The alternative is to head back through the slot and swim through the cave back to the bay. The cave is eerie and don't be surprised if you come across the odd seal. There are several exit points as you exit the cave which lead back to the main path.

Black head

Black Head is the headland poking out from the small village of Trenarren. This is a very tranquil place and large groups should avoid it to keep it this way. The headland holds the majority of interest for coasteering but the surrounding area also has much to offer.

Approach

Get on the A390 and drive towards St. Austell. Follow signs for Porthpean and turn off onto Porthpean Road, which also takes you to the Hospital. Drive for 2 miles passing the Hospital and the Golf Course. Turn left at a small crossroads towards Trenarren. There is a small free car park just before you enter the village.
Where the road splits, walk down the left hand road which meets the big coastal path towards Blackhead. When you reach the headland take the left track and pick your way through the narrow path that cuts left towards a small scramble and the get in.

Entry	Exit	Car Park	Post Code
SX 039 482	SX 038 480	SX 033 490	PL26 6BH

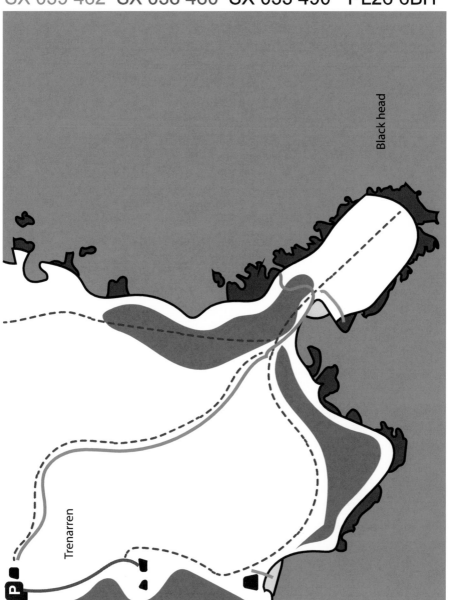

Description

This trip is possible at most states of the tide but I recommend going near low - mid tide. The jumps are bigger, the climbs more rewarding and the caves are more impressive. Start off by scrambling the first 50m where some easy climbing gets you to the top of several enjoyable jumps. At low water the landing areas shrink so choose wisely. Continue swimming and climbing around to a small canyon like zawn. Jumping into this is frightening because of the narrow 2m landing area but the take off is solid. As you continue around the headland make the most of the easy jumps and some challenging traversing.

The tip of Blackhead is popular with fishing and it is easy to access or egress the sea from here. Scramble along the small ledges for 50m and you will reach a large zawn with a cave. The cave is worth an explore and as you look at the cave you will notice a big 10-12m jumping ledge on your left. This is reachable by climbing up the left hand side of the ledge. This jump requires a clean landing to prevent any injuries. It's also a long swim/scramble out, so take this into consideration before you jump. The final side of the headland has long stretches of good sea level traversing for all abilities and small fun jumping all the way along. Blackhead ends in a small bay where you can easily get to the main path back to the car. It's not over yet though. A short swim across the bay rewards you with a spit of land with 8-10m jumps from wide safe ledges into deep water.

West Cornwall

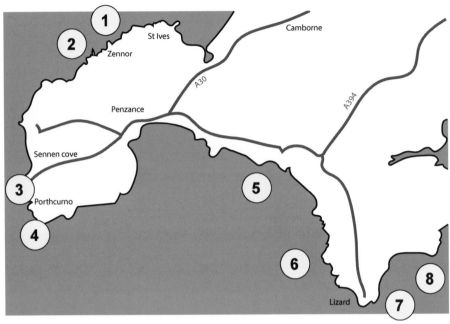

The far west of Cornwall has some of the most scenic
coasteering in the country. In a short drive you can access the
north and south coast, giving you options in rough conditions.
The variety of wildlife in the region brings an exciting aspect
to the venues. This is a small section of what is on offer in the
area. Use this guide as a starting point and then enjoy exploring
all that West Cornwall has to offer.

Zennor Head

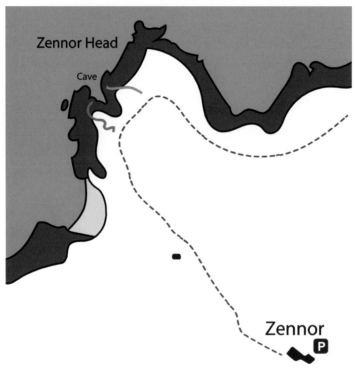

Zennor is a small village west of St Ives with a great pub and easy parking. The trip is short but the scenery and volume of features in such a small space make it a classic and exposed coasteering venue.

Approach

The village has a small car park with toilets next to a bunkhouse. Travelling on the B3306, Zennor is 5.5 miles from St Ives or 8.7 miles from St Just. The coastal path is reached via the road leading towards the headland. Pass the luxurious looking houses and the road turns into a footpath. Follow this up onto the headland and along the cliffs until you see a grassy slope with an old granite boundary marker. Descend the slope passing the zawn and onto the rock ledges.

Description

The initial slab has some good warm up jumps on. Make the most out of these as the rest are above 6m. The big zawn is where most of the action is. Looking down the zawn into the eerie cave you will see ledges up and to your left. The big jumps are here and can be accessed via some difficult climbing. The rock is barnacle free so it is very slippery - the first person up could set up a hand line to help. There are sunken rocks in the zawn but the gaps between them are extremely deep. The cave is dangerous in any swell. The sea speeds up and gains height in the constriction and there are person shape holes which you would not want to get stuck in. Exploring the area around the zawn does hold some interest if you want to extend your trip. There are other ways of climbing out but the descent path is your safest ascent path too.

Boswednack

Boswednack Cliffs sit opposite Gurnards Head which is famous for its climbing and walking. This is a 'must do' coasteering trip if you're in the region. The trip is made up of imposing cliffs and smaller islands that are separated by slots and gullies. Expect narrow landings, wide caves and immense jumps.

Approach

Park at The Gurnards Head Hotel which is on the B3306 half way between St Just and St Ives. If you're not going to eat or drink here there is parking opposite on a small grassy area. Follow the road down through the few houses and farms then follow signs for the public footpath and Gurnards Head. The path takes you across some open fields and on towards the headland. Before you reach the headland the path turns east, past a ruined tower and a large house. An easy descent brings you to the sea.

Entry	Exit	Car Park	Post Code
SW 436 383	SW 440 386	SW 436 376	TR26 3DE

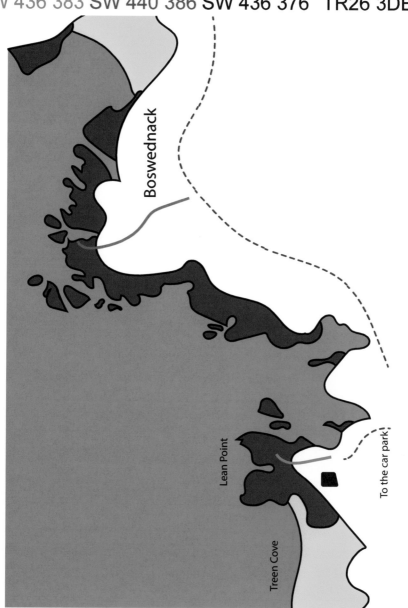

Boswednack

Lean Point

Treen Cove

To the car park

Description

An immediate 3m jump off Lean Point and a small swim into the bay start the trip. Pick your landings between the rocks on the next few jumps then move onto the first island. Swim through the gully created by the island and climb up either side to access fun 3-5m jumps into the fairly narrow landing zone. The landings are clear and deep but over jumping will take you dangerously close to the opposite wall. Climb up onto to the next ledges and you will find a labyrinth of narrow fissures that lead through and under the rock. The best way to not miss anything is to scout from above and then enter through one of the narrow slots. The main slot is around 4m deep at high tide and can be jumped into. Warning, this is not very wide and a miss judged jump could have serious consequences.

 More exploration will lead you to the next island which is separated from the mainland by a 10m channel. Intimidating 10-12m jumps lie on either side - choose your landings wisely because there is not much room for error. As the gap narrows the slot gets very shallow which can cause some powerful swell surges. The two big caves don't go back very deep but are still an eerie place to go and explore. Further around the headland you will find lots of small rock islands with jumps and crevasses to amuse you. The biggest island that stands alone has a fantastic 6m jump on its seaward side. The exit point is in the next zawn and it is a series of cave like holes. Look up and right from in the zawn and you will see two distinct holes which have had water running through them at some point. Climb up and through the first hole and a short but steep climb brings you to the second one. This is a tight squeeze that exits right on the cliff edge. From here pick your way up the ridge avoiding the big sump holes until you reach the coastal path. This can get overgrown so expect to do some bushwhacking.

Porthgwarra

Porthgwarra is a small but scenic village just North of Porthcurno. The village has a cafe, toilets and parking. The coasteering here is impressive. The rock formations and high imposing cliffs give you a real sense of adventure and exploration. All this is over seen by the Coastwatch tower.

Approach

Drive towards Lands End from Penzance on the A30. The A30 ends at Sennen. Turn onto the B3315 signposted to Porthcurno and the Minack Theatre. 2 miles later you enter a small village and on the sharp left hand bend turn right, following signs for Porthgwarra. When you enter the village follow parking signs and pay your money in the cafe - bring some change. You can get an idea of the conditions from the beach, if it is all good then head up the steep coastal path towards the Coastwatch Tower. Before the tower you will see the big fennel hole which is a collapsed cave. The ridge just past the hole is the entry point.

Entry   Exit   Car Park   Post Code

SW 366 215   SW 371 216   SW 371 217   TR19 6JR

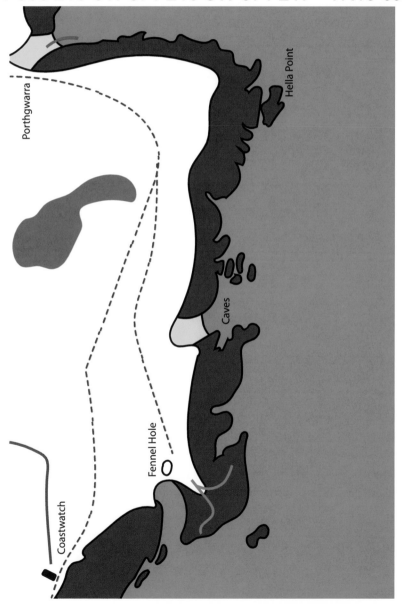

Description

The big fennel hole marks the entry point for this trip. Looking back along the route you will get an idea of how committing the route is. Flat conditions are best for this trip. Go past the hole and onto the ridge of rock that summits the small headland. You can pick your way down here - it is not as steep as it looks from the top. Head down the Westward side of the headland and you can see some small gullies across the bay. These are worth swimming too, as the 3m jumps are a good warm up. Come back on yourself and start scrambling East around the headland until you get to a small bay. The bottom of the fennel hole is here and if you climb up to the collapsed cave entrance you will see the light peeping down and fresh rock fall within - don't get any closer. Jump into the crystal clear water and swim into the bay. There is a small cave entrance up above. Although it is too tight to fit in it is worth a look as you can see if there are any seals in the cave below. Scramble round at sea level and you will see the two cave entrances. They form a kind of skull shape in the rock. Head in and take a look, keeping an eye out for seals.

Swim across to a series of rock towers that come out of the sea. A tricky climb can get you to the top of both towers where you can jump the 8m's back down. There is only small landing areas between the sunken rocks, you need clear conditions to spot your landing. You can see the next feature ahead, a large island on Hella Point. On the way there enjoy the small jumps and fantastic traversing. There is an escape route here that leads you back to the coastal path. On the point is a narrow gap between the mainland and the island. The cliffs are huge and tower over you while you swim towards them. The island has some narrow 3m jumps on the seaward side but the highlight is jumping 10m from the island ridge down into the narrow gully. Swim through the gully to start your way inland towards the beach. You will find a few small jumps on the way but things calm down as you get to the beach. The car park is 50m walk from the beach.

Porthcurno

Porthcurno is home to the Telegraph Museum, the Minack Theatre and an extremely popular beach. If that's not enough to entice you, the coasteering is excellent too. The guide describes the trip from Porthchapel to Porthcurno but it is just as good the other way round. The trip scenery is fantastic and it is full of jumps, climbs and a long sump.

Approach

From Penzance follow the A30 West. 6 miles before Land's End take the B3283 signposted Porthcurno and the Minack Theatre. Follow this road for 6 miles and take the well signed road to Porthcurno. I recommend continuing on to St Leven, past the Minack and parking at the Parish Car Park. It's cheaper and supports the local community. From here follow the signs to the beach. There has been some erosion on the path near the beach so look out for the signed danger spots. You can then walk back from Porthcurno via the road or the coastal path .

		3		
1.5km	500m 1km		1m 12m	
Entry	**Exit**	**Car Park**	**Post Code**	
SW 436 383	SW 440 386	SW 436 376	PL26	

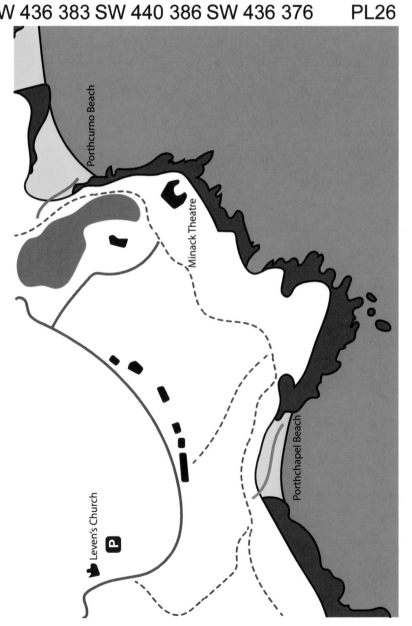

Description

From the beach rock hop along towards the small islands known as the Carracks. It's fun navigating through the huge boulders and there are plenty of holes to explore and crawl through. The odd gap between the sunken boulders is deep enough to jump into, so keep your eye out for take off ledges. The small islands are riddled with shallow pits and ledges to swim around and a 30m swim to the biggest island will reward you with a 6m jump from the top. The next feature is a narrow but extremely deep zawn. The jumps range from 3 -10m and the take off ledges are on both sides. The next smaller zawn is still deep and has a 6m jump from a solid take off. Keep traversing along on large boulders with small fun jumps until you can see the bay. Just before you cross the bay there is a narrow crack guarded by a suspended boulder. You can swim under this into a tall chamber where there is a second rock to duck under and into a cave. The sumps are 3m long and it is important that you check under the boulders for any obstacles. Swim across the bay and admire the big gaping hole in the cliffs. This is surrounded by fallen rocks so I wouldn't recommend going in there.

After the bay is a series of small zawns which lead under the Minack theatre. Each one has a jump, although the landings on some are quite narrow because of fallen rocks which hide under the water. If you get a flat day then the viability is usually great so you can spot the dangers. The narrow drops tests your accuracy and all the folks at the theatre give you an audience. As you reach the headland you will see a pointy overhanging rock which is the take off for an amazing 8m jump. The landing is tight because the sides scoop out forming a small gully. Swim under the jump, climb up and traverse the small ledges to reach the pointy rock. After this move round towards the beach. This section is mostly rock hopping until you reach a sloping ledge with 3 jumping points on it. Finish up on the beach and either walk back along the road or the coastal path back to St Leven.

Trewavas Head

Trewavas Head is the headland just south of Rinsey Head. Rinsey Head is popular with climbers and is home to one of the UKs largest Kittiwake population. If you're after big jumps without too much exposure or hassle then this is an ideal location for you. Although exciting in rough conditions, the small zawns become dangerous and the jumps are hard to time correctly.

Approach

The turning for Rinsey is 2 miles past Praa Sands on the A394. Drive a mile down Rinsey Lane and you will come to the big National Trust Car Park. Change here and follow the track down past the ruin and continue along the footpath. Either start from the beach of carry on the path to start nearer the action.

Entry	**Exit**	**Car Park**	**Post Code**
SW 594 267	SW 596 264	SW 591 271	TR13 9TS

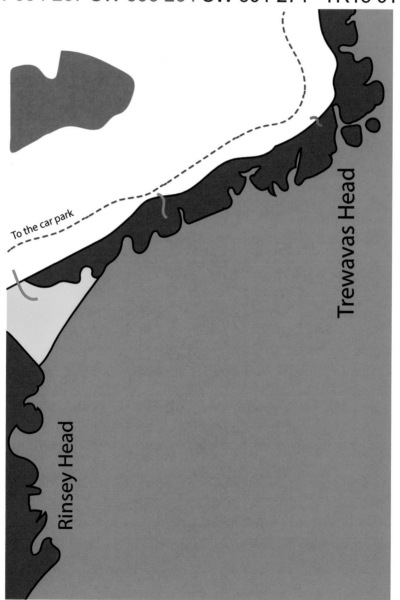

To the car park

Trewavas Head

Rinsey Head

Description

If you have started from the beach then enjoy the scrambling and small jumps before you get to the inlet with a narrow gully. Alternately scramble down to here from the footpath. The jumps start straight away. Rock hop or swim your way to the first big jump. You will see a large flat block with a big ledge on top. This 6-8m jump has an easy take off and a deep landing but the rocks directly below the jump can be off putting. This is a fantastic jump to practise technique and to repeat over and over. From the landing pool you enter a gorge like gully which narrows until you can climb out of it. Hours of fun are to be had here, jumping from the numerous ledges and getting washed around if there is any swell. Scramble over the slabs to the next zawn, where a 6m jump will get you back into the water. A short swim or traverse will bring to the largest zawn with the biggest jumps.

You can jump from pretty much anywhere you can climb up to. The biggest jump is set back into the zawn and can be reached by climbing up in the crack. This is 10m high and not for the beginner as you have to jump out over a jumble of rocks to reach the deep landing. A slip or misjudged jump here would be very bad indeed. You can continue exploring around the corner but it gets more difficult to get out and the features slacken off. The easiest way to exit is to climb up out of the zawn and join the main track back.

Kynance Cove

This hugely popular tourist site has a café and plenty of parking. It is maintained by the National Trust and has a well defined track to the cove. To enjoy all this venue has to offer you need to be here on a calm day. Swell is exaggerated by the contrasting depth and the positioning of the islands. The islands are also riddled with caves for the sea to push and suck through. Expect a lot of people to be watching and look out for the odd basking shark.

Approach

Drive down the A3083 towards the Lizard. About 1.5 miles beforehand turn right down the well signposted road towards Kynance cove. The car park is 1 mile down the road. Park up and follow the signs and obvious footpath towards the cove. Get in below the café.

Entry / Exit
SW 684 133

800m 400m 400m 3

Car Park
SW 688 133

0.5m 12m

Post Code
TR12 7PJ

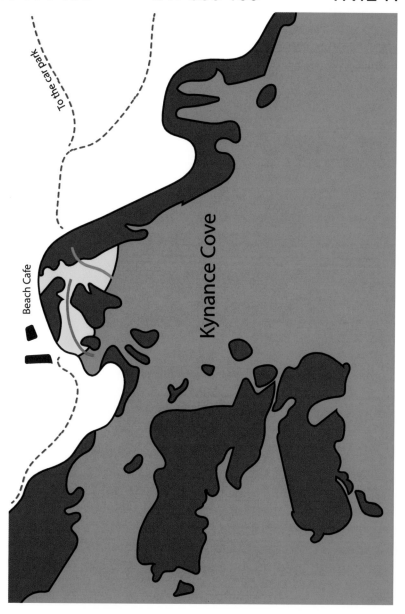

To the car park

Beach Cafe

Kynance Cove

Description

Looking out to sea from below the café, most of the action is towards your right. Many of the small islands have good warm up jumps to get you started. The tallest of these initial islands has a nervy 6m jump into shallow water. 50m further on you will reach a sandbar which connects the main islands to the mainland. Swell hits this from both sides and you get some unusual currents that can be fun to play in. Past the sandbar is two tall conical islands. Both have decent jumping points at high water, although the climbs to reach them are difficult. Keep an eye out for the seals that love playing here as much as we do. A big slab joins two of the main islands here, forming a small groove where one island rests on the other. Under this groove is a long underwater cave which goes through to the other side of the islands. As the sea moves up and down, air is sucked into the cave and then pushed out making strange demon like noises. This blow hole is know as the Devils Bellows.

Climb up the slab and through the groove to gain some height and reach the summit of the biggest island. The view from here is amazing and you feel isolated compared with the masses eating ice-cream opposite. Scramble over the island's ridge towards the sea and the convergence of the three largest islands. Down climb a little and jump the 10m into the wide gulley created by the meeting of the islands. At low tide this gully can be too shallow to jump into. Being in the gulley, surrounded by huge cliffs is an experience you will remember and repeat. There are loads of features to play around in here, you could even climb back up to the entry jump and do it again. Swim out the gully and start heading right to continue around the island. The first feature you will come across is a fantastic deep zawn that leads into a narrow cave.

The cave ends with a large opening up above you. If you were to climb out you would end up perched 4m up and facing the cafe and beach. The jumps here are some of the best. As you look down the zawn you will notice two ideal ledges 12m above and to your right. Easy climbing gets you up to these exciting jumps which land in the narrowest part of the zawn. Opposite these is another 12m jump from a big wide ledge. Unfortunately the climb up is intimidating and a fall would be serious. Next is a smaller zawn with a shallow ledge where the sea washes up and creates some fun features. This is where the Devil's Bellows comes out, a long swim underwater even with a tank on. There are a few good 6m jumps to do here before you move on. From here continue round the island back to the sand bar. Alternately swim back through the gully and explore the West side of the islands. If you go this way you will see the exit hole to the narrow cave up above.

For an extended trip explore the most Southern island. This is a fantastic circumnavigation mainly due to the large deep bay cut into it. Getting to the bay is largely swimming and easy scrambling but it is worth it. Jumps surround the sides of the harbour like bay and you could spend a lot of time here before the quick jaunt back to the beach.

Church Cove

Church Cove is a sheltered short venue which is jam packed with fun features. Life boats are launched from here and the RNLI have a Visitors Centre which I highly recommend visiting. The cove itself only has a handful of houses which are likely to invoke jealousy from most of us. The parking is limited and the area is peaceful so please respect the local inhabitants.

Approach

Drive towards the Lizard on the A3083. Half a mile before the Lizard and just after a lay by full of recycling bins you will see a left turn signposted Church Cove and Housel Bay. Follow the road into the cove and park at the Church. Get changed and follow the road on the left towards the RNLI Station.

Entry	Exit	Car Park	Post Code
SW 715 125	SW 714 127	SW 711 126	TR12 7PH

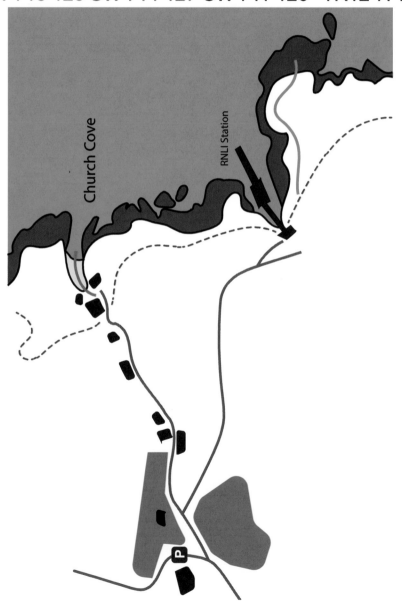

Description

Walk past the RNLI Station and turn left by the bench onto the track. This leads to a small headland which is a popular fishing spot. Enter the water from any one of the small ledges here. Alternately jump straight in from the 8m jump which faces the station, an exciting initial entry. Rather than just swimming across the bay, traverse along the wall until it you reach the life boat ramp and jump in from a small slab. Please do not climb on the ramp and beware that this is a busy station. Swim under the ramp and head around to the small inlet. There are plenty of 2-5m jumps in this section as well as my favourite feature, the sump. In the narrow gully formed by a small island of rock is a suspended boulder which forms the sump. You can push yourself down under it and use your hands to propel yourself to the other side, following the light.

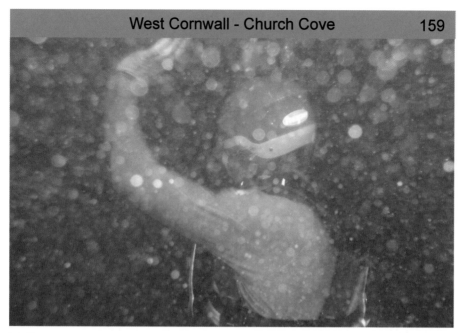

Follow on and make the most out of the small slots, mini islands and a 4-5m jump just before you move into the cove itself.

It's not over yet. Swim across the cove and note the ledges dotted around the cliff face. At high tide it is deep here and you can pick and choose from the many possible jumping spots. If you want a bit more, then head out of the cove and continue around the point. There is a small but fun jump here as well as a cauldron like pit. At the entrance of this, is a narrow gap which forces the water though with a surprising amount of power. The terrain changes from here on so head back the way you came and swim up to the jetty in the cove. Walk back up the road, admiring the plush houses until you reach the car park.

Cadgwith Cove

Cadgwith is a picturesque Cornish fishing village on the sheltered side of the Lizard. The village has a pub, shop and a restaurant so finding food and a drink afterwards is easy enough. The trip takes you around the south hand side of the cove and gives you a chance to see the impressive Devil's Frying Pan close up rather than from the coastal path. This trip is a good option if the other side of the Lizard is too rough.

Approach

Drive down the A3083 towards the Lizard. Just after the Predannack Airfield, about 2 miles from the Lizard turn left onto the country road signposted Cadgwith. Keep following signs for 1.5 miles until you reach the large car park. Walk down the little track signposted for the village. You will see a small spit of land with a bench on it and steps down to the sea.

| 800m | 500m | 1.3km | | | | 0.5m | 12m |

Entry   **Exit**   **Car Park**   **Post Code**

SW 722 145   SW 720 139   SW 719 148   TR12 7JZ

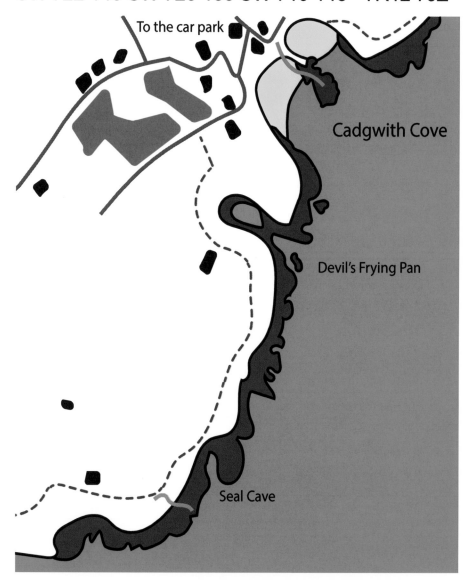

To the car park

Cadgwith Cove

Devil's Frying Pan

Seal Cave

Description

Swim across the bay and start traversing out of the cove. Immediately you will come across 3 jumps and easy climbing. Around the corner you will find the first little island separated by a 4m gap from the headland. Hidden rocks mean you will have to be accurate on your landings while jumping from here. The next feature is the atmospheric Devil's Frying Pan. This was formed when a cave collapsed leaving a huge hole and a rock arch. Swim through the arch into the collapsed cave and wave to the walkers up on the path. Opposite the frying pan is the next small island which has numerous jumps ranging between 2m and 6m - the slab style climbing is also great fun. Scramble through the small gap in the 20m rock tower or if your too big, climb over the jumble of rocks and into the zawn. The seaward side of the tower has a large ledge to jump into the narrow zawn from. Traverse around the tower and climb up onto a series of ledges to reach it. There is also a small cave here which is fun to squeeze into.

Climb around the corner and into the large inlet which has a huge cave in the back of it. Quite often this cave is home to seals which makes the 10m swim across the cave entrance more exciting. The cave goes in a long way, around 70m. The further you go in, the darker and narrower it gets until you reach the spooky beach in the back. As you enter the cave there are a few excellent 6-8m jumps on the right hand side. After the cave is a sloping face leading to the exit and the biggest jumps of the trip are also from here. Climb up the slope and traverse left to find a solid ledge 12m up. If you still have some energy then keep going and you will find a small pool like bay. It is worth it for the small but enjoyable jumps and an amazing view of the Lizard. Head back to the exit where you're path lies up through the rocks and over the rock ridge that leads to the top. If you go off track here you will be waist high in gorse, follow the ridge. The scramble out is high and exposed and it may not be for everyone. You could always return to the cove by going back along the cliffs if your team don't fancy it.

Printed in Great Britain
by Amazon